GRADE **K**

Mindset Mathematics

Visualizing and Investigating Big Ideas

Jo Boaler

Jen Munson

Cathy Williams

JB JOSSEY-BASS™
A Wiley Brand

Published by Jossey-Bass
A Wiley Brand
111 River St, Hoboken, NJ 07030
www.josseybass.com

Jossey-Bass books and products are available through most bookstores. To contact Jossey-Bass directly call our Customer Care Department within the U.S. at 800-956-7739, outside the U.S. at 317-572-3986, or fax 317-572-4002.

Wiley publishes in a variety of print and electronic formats and by print-on-demand. Some material included with standard print versions of this book may not be included in e-books or in print-on-demand. If this book refers to media such as a CD or DVD that is not included in the version you purchased, you may download this material at http://booksupport.wiley.com. For more information about Wiley products, visit www.wiley.com.

The Visualize, Play, and Investigate icons are used under license from Shutterstock.com and the following arists: Blan-k, Marish, and SuzanaM.

Library of Congress Cataloging-in-Publication Data

Names: Boaler, Jo, 1964- author. | Munson, Jen, 1977- author. | Williams,
    Cathy, 1962- author.
Title: Mindset mathematics : visualizing and investigating big ideas, grade
    K / Jo Boaler, Jen Munson, Cathy Williams.
Description: Hoboken, NJ : Jossey-Bass, 2020. | Includes index.
Identifiers: LCCN 2020008315 (print) | LCCN 2020008316 (ebook) | ISBN
    9781119357605 (paperback) | ISBN 9781119358596 (adobe pdf) | ISBN
    9781119358602 (epub)
Subjects: LCSH: Games in mathematics education. | Mathematics—Study and
    teaching (Elementary)—Activity programs. | Kindergarten.
Classification: LCC QA20.G35 B6388 2020 (print) | LCC QA20.G35 (ebook) |
    DDC 372.7/049—dc23
LC record available at https://lccn.loc.gov/2020008315
LC ebook record available at https://lccn.loc.gov/2020008316

Cover design by Wiley
Cover images: eye © Marish/Shutterstock, background © Kritchanut/iStockphoto, line drawing © Wiley
Printed in the United States of America

FIRST EDITION

PB Printing   SKY10034650_060222

Contents

To all those teachers pursuing a mathematical mindset journey with us.

Introduction

I still remember the moment when Youcubed, the Stanford center I direct, was conceived. I was at the Denver NCSM and NCTM conferences in 2013, and I had arranged to meet Cathy Williams, the director of mathematics for Vista Unified School District. Cathy and I had been working together for the past year improving mathematics teaching in her district. We had witnessed amazing changes taking place, and a filmmaker had documented some of the work. I had recently released my online teacher course, called How to Learn Math, and been overwhelmed by requests from tens of thousands of teachers to provide them with more of the same ideas. Cathy and I decided to create a website and use it to continue sharing the ideas we had used in her district and that I had shared in my online class. Soon after we started sharing ideas on the Youcubed website, we were invited to become a Stanford University center, and Cathy became the codirector of the center with me.

In the months that followed, with the help of one of my undergraduates, Montse Cordero, our first version of youcubed.org was launched. By January 2015, we had managed to raise some money and hire engineers, and we launched a revised version of the site that is close to the site you may know today. We were very excited that in the first month of that relaunch, we had five thousand visits to the site. At the time of writing this, we are now getting three million visits to the site each month. Teachers are excited to learn about the new research and to take the tools, videos, and activities that translate research ideas into practice and use them in their teaching.

Low-Floor, High-Ceiling Tasks

One of the most popular articles on our website is called "Fluency without Fear." I wrote this with Cathy when I heard from many teachers that they were being made to use timed tests in the elementary grades. At the same time, new brain science was emerging showing that when people feel stressed—as students do when facing a timed test—part of their brain, the working memory, is restricted. The working memory is exactly the area of the brain that comes into play when students need to calculate with math facts, and this is the exact area that is impeded when students are stressed. We have evidence now that suggests strongly that timed math tests in the early grades are responsible for the early onset of math anxiety for many students. I teach an undergraduate class at Stanford, and many of the undergraduates are math traumatized. When I ask them what happened to cause this, almost all of them will recall, with startling clarity, the time in elementary school when they were given timed tests. We are really pleased that "Fluency without Fear" has now been used across the United States to pull timed tests out of school districts. It has been downloaded many thousands of times and used in state and national hearings.

One of the reasons for the amazing success of the paper is that it does not just share the brain science on the damage of timed tests but also offers an alternative to timed tests: activities that teach math facts conceptually and through activities that students and teachers enjoy. One of the activities—a game called How Close to 100—became so popular that thousands of teachers tweeted photos of their students playing the game. There was so much attention on Twitter and other media that Stanford noticed and decided to write a news story on the damage of speed to mathematics learning. This was picked up by news outlets across the United States, including *US News & World Report,* which is part of the reason the white paper has now had so many downloads and so much impact. Teachers themselves caused this mini revolution by spreading news of the activities and research.

How Close to 100 is just one of many tasks we have on youcubed.org that are extremely popular with teachers and students. All our tasks have the feature of being "low floor and high ceiling," which I consider to be an extremely important quality for engaging all students in a class. If you are teaching only one student, then a mathematics task can be fairly narrow in terms of its content and difficulty. But whenever you have a group of students, there will be differences in their needs, and they will be challenged by different ideas. A low-floor, high-ceiling task is one in which everyone can engage, no matter what his or her prior understanding or knowledge, but also one that is open enough to extend to high levels, so that all students can be deeply challenged. In the last two years, we have launched an introductory week of mathematics lessons on our site that are open, visual, and low floor, high ceiling. These have been extremely popular with teachers; they have had approximately four million downloads and are used in 20% of schools across the United States.

In our extensive work with teachers around the United States, we are continually asked for more tasks that are like those on our website. Most textbook publishers seem to ignore or be unaware of research on mathematics learning, and most textbook questions are narrow and insufficiently engaging for students. It is imperative that the new knowledge of the ways our brains learn mathematics is incorporated into the lessons students are given in classrooms. It is for this reason that we chose to write a series of books that are organized around a principle of active student engagement, that reflect the latest brain science on learning, and that include activities that are low floor and high ceiling.

Youcubed Summer Camp

We recently brought 81 students onto the Stanford campus for a Youcubed summer math camp, to teach them in the ways that are encouraged in this book. We used open, creative, and visual math tasks. After only 18 lessons with us, the students improved their test score performance by an average of 50%, the equivalent of 1.6 years of school. More important, they changed their relationship with mathematics and started believing in their own potential. They did this, in part, because we talked to them about the brain science showing that

- There is no such thing as a math person—anyone can learn mathematics to high levels.
- Mistakes, struggle, and challenge are critical for brain growth.
- Speed is unimportant in mathematics.
- Mathematics is a visual and beautiful subject, and our brains want to think visually about mathematics.

All of these messages were key to the students' changed mathematics relationship, but just as critical were the tasks we worked on in class. The tasks and the messages about the brain were perfect complements to each other, as we told students they could learn anything, and we showed them a mathematics that was open, creative, and engaging. This approach helped them see that they could learn mathematics and actually do so. This book shares the kinds of tasks that we used in our summer camp, that make up our week of inspirational mathematics (WIM) lessons, and that we post on our site.

Before I outline and introduce the different sections of the book and the ways we are choosing to engage students, I will share some important ideas about how students learn mathematics.

Memorization versus Conceptual Engagement

Many students get the wrong idea about mathematics—exactly the wrong idea. Through years of mathematics classes, many students come to believe that their role in mathematics learning is to memorize methods and facts, and that mathematics success comes from memorization. I say this is exactly the wrong idea because there is actually very little to remember in mathematics. The subject is made up of a few big, linked ideas, and students who are successful in mathematics are those who see the subject as a set of ideas that they need to think deeply about. The Program for International Student Assessment (PISA) tests are international assessments of mathematics, reading, and science that are given every three years. In 2012, PISA not only assessed mathematics achievement but also collected data on students' approach to mathematics. I worked with the PISA team in Paris at the Organisation for Economic Co-operation and Development (OECD) to analyze students' mathematics approaches and their relationship to achievement. One clear result emerged from this analysis. Students approached mathematics in three distinct ways. One group approached mathematics by attempting to memorize the methods they had met; another group took a "relational" approach, relating new concepts to those they already knew; and a third group took a self-monitoring approach, thinking about what they knew and needed to know.

In every country, the memorizers were the lowest-achieving students, and countries with high numbers of memorizers were all lower achieving. In no country were memorizers in the highest-achieving group, and in some high-achieving countries such as Japan, students who combined self-monitoring and relational strategies outscored memorizing students by more than a year's worth of schooling. More detail on this finding is given in this *Scientific American* Mind article that I coauthored with a PISA analyst: https://www.scientificamerican.com/article/ why-math-education-in-the-u-s-doesn-t-add-up/.

Mathematics is a conceptual subject, and it is important for students to be thinking slowly, deeply, and conceptually about mathematical ideas, not racing through methods that they try to memorize. One reason that students need to think conceptually has to do with the ways the brain processes mathematics. When we learn new mathematical ideas, they take up a large space in our brain as the brain works out where they fit and what they connect with. But with time, as we move on with our understanding, the knowledge becomes compressed in the brain, taking up a very small space. For first graders, the idea of addition takes up a large space in their brains as they think about how it works and what it means, but for adults the idea of addition is compressed, and it takes up a small space. When adults are asked to add 2 and 3, for example, they can quickly and easily extract the compressed knowledge. William Thurston (1990), a mathematician who won the Field's Medal—the highest honor in mathematics—explains compression like this:

> Mathematics is amazingly compressible: you may struggle a long time, step by step, to work through the same process or idea from several approaches. But once you really understand it and have the mental perspective to see it as a whole, there is often a tremendous mental compression. You can file it away, recall it quickly and completely when you need it, and use it as just one step in some other mental process. The insight that goes with this compression is one of the real joys of mathematics.

You will probably agree with me that not many students think of mathematics as a "real joy," and part of the reason is that they are not compressing mathematical ideas in their brain. This is because the brain only compresses concepts, not methods. So if students are thinking that mathematics is a set of methods to memorize, they are on the wrong pathway, and it is critical that we change that. It is very important that students think deeply and conceptually about ideas. We provide the activities in this book that will allow students to think deeply and conceptually, and an essential role of the teacher is to give the students time to do so.

Mathematical Thinking, Reasoning, and Convincing

When we worked with our Youcubed camp students, we gave each of them journals to record their mathematical thinking. I am a big fan of journaling—for myself and my students. For mathematics students, it helps show them that mathematics is a subject for which we should record ideas and pictures. We can use journaling to encourage students to keep organized records, which is another important part of mathematics, and help them understand that mathematical thinking can be a long and slow process. Journals also give students free space—where they can be creative, share ideas, and feel ownership of their work. We did not write in the students' journals, as we wanted them to think of the journals as their space, not something that teachers wrote on. We gave students feedback on sticky notes that we stuck onto their work. The images in Figure I.1 show some of the mathematical records the camp students kept in their journals.

Another resource I always share with learners is the act of color-coding—that is, students using colors to highlight different ideas. For example, when working on an algebraic task, they may show the *x* in the same color in an expression, in a graph, and in a picture, as shown in Figure I.2. When adding numbers, color-coding may help show the addends (Figure I.3).

Color-coding highlights connections, which are a really critical part of mathematics.

Another important part of mathematics is the act of reasoning—explaining why methods are chosen and how steps are linked, and using logic to connect ideas.

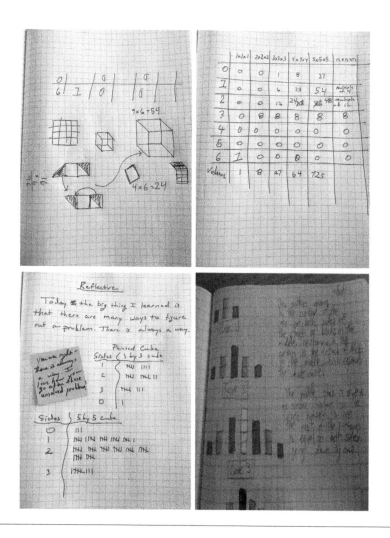

Figure I.1

Mindset Mathematics, Grade K

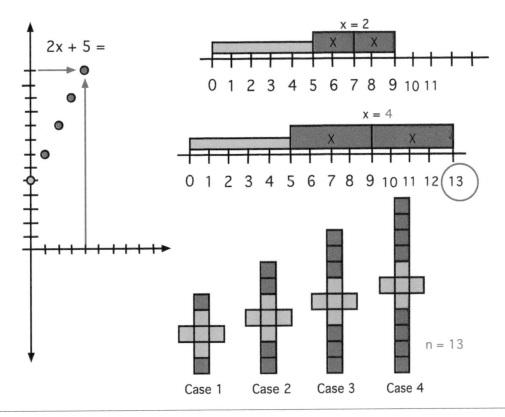

Figure I.2

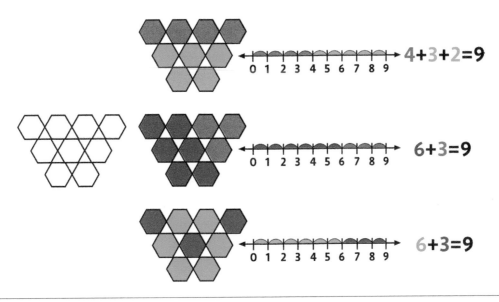

Figure I.3

Reasoning is at the heart of mathematics. Scientists prove ideas by finding more cases that fit a theory, or countercases that contradict a theory, but mathematicians prove their work by reasoning. If students are not reasoning, then they are not really doing mathematics. In the activities of these books, we suggest a framework that encourages students to be convincing when they reason. We tell them that there are three levels of being convincing. The first, or easiest, level is to convince yourself of something. A higher level is to convince a friend. And the highest level of all is to convince a skeptic. We also share with students that they should be skeptics with one another, asking one another why methods were chosen and how they work. We have found this framework to be very powerful with students; they enjoy being skeptics, pushing each other to deeper levels of reasoning, and it encourages students to reason clearly, which is important for their learning.

We start each book in our series with an activity that invites students to reason about mathematics and be convincing. I first met an activity like this when reading Mark Driscoll's teaching ideas in his book *Fostering Algebraic Thinking*. I thought it was a perfect activity for introducing the skeptics framework that I had learned from a wonderful teacher, Cathy Humphreys. She had learned about and adapted the framework from two of my inspirational teachers from England: mathematician John Mason and mathematics educator Leone Burton. As well as encouraging students to be convincing, in a number of activities we ask students to prove an idea. Some people think of proof as a formal set of steps that they learned in geometry class. But the act of proving is really about connecting ideas, and as students enter the learning journey of proving, it is worthwhile celebrating their steps toward formal proof. Mathematician Paul Lockhart (2012) rejects the idea that proving is about following a set of formal steps, instead proposing that proving is "abstract art, pure and simple. And art is always a struggle. There is no systematic way of creating beautiful and meaningful paintings or sculptures, and there is also no method for producing beautiful and meaningful mathematical arguments" (p. 8). Instead of suggesting that students follow formal steps, we invite them to think deeply about mathematical concepts and make connections. Students will be given many ways to be creative when they prove and justify, and for reasons I discuss later, we always encourage and celebrate visual as well as numerical and algebraic justifications. Ideally, students will create visual, numerical, and algebraic representations and connect their ideas through color-coding and through verbal explanations. Students are excited to experience mathematics in these ways, and they benefit from the opportunity to bring their individual ideas and creativity to the problem-solving and learning space. As students develop in their mathematical understanding, we can encourage them to extend and generalize their ideas through reasoning, justifying, and proving. This process deepens their understanding and helps them compress their learning.

Big Ideas

The books in the Mindset Mathematics Series are all organized around mathematical "big ideas." Mathematics is not a set of methods; it is a set of connected ideas that need to be understood. When students understand the big ideas in mathematics, the methods and rules fall into place. One of the reasons any set of curriculum standards is flawed is that standards take the beautiful subject of mathematics and its many connections, and divide it into small pieces that make the connections disappear. Instead of starting with the small pieces, we have started with the big ideas and important connections, and have listed the relevant Common Core curriculum standards within the activities. Our activities invite students to engage in the mathematical acts that are listed in the imperative Common Core practice standards, and they also teach many of the Common Core content standards, which emerge from the rich activities. Student activity pages are noted with a ☉ and teacher activity pages are noted with a ⊕.

Although we have chapters for each big idea, as though they are separate from each other, they are all intrinsically linked. Figure I.4 shows some of the connections between the ideas, and you may be able to see others. It is very important to share with students that mathematics is a subject of connections and to highlight the connections as students work. You may want to print the color visual of the different connections for students to see as they work. To see the maps of big ideas for all of the grades K through 8, find our paper "What Is Mathematical Beauty?" at youcubed.org.

Structure of the Book

Visualize. Play. Investigate. These three words provide the structure for each book in the series. They also pave the way for open student thinking, for powerful brain connections, for engagement, and for deep understanding. How do they do that? And why is this book so different from other mathematics curriculum books?

Visualize ◉

For the past few years, I have been working with a neuroscience group at Stanford, under the direction of Vinod Menon, which specializes in mathematics learning. We have been working together to think about the ways that findings from brain science can be used to help learners of mathematics. One of the exciting discoveries that has

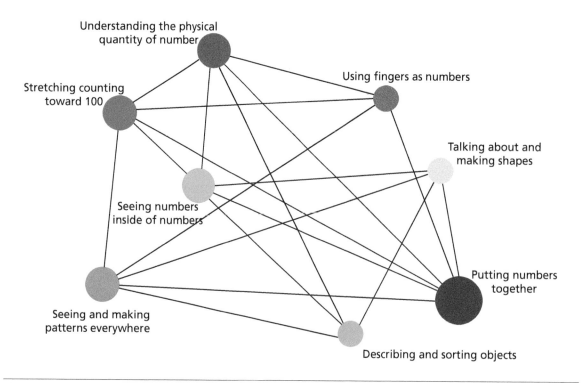

Understanding the physical
quantity of number

Using fingers as numbers

Stretching counting
toward 100

Talking about and
making shapes

Seeing numbers
inside of numbers

Putting numbers
together

Seeing and making
patterns everywhere

Describing and sorting objects

Figure I.4

been emerging over the last few years is the importance of visualizing for the brain and our learning of mathematics. Brain scientists now know that when we work on mathematics, even when we perform a bare number calculation, five areas of the brain are involved, as shown in Figure I.5.

Two of the five brain pathways—the dorsal and ventral pathways—are visual. The dorsal visual pathway is the main brain region for representing quantity. This may seem surprising, as so many of us have sat through hundreds of hours of mathematics classes working with numbers, while barely ever engaging visually with mathematics. Now brain scientists know that our brains "see" fingers when we calculate, and knowing fingers well—what they call finger perception—is critical for the development of an understanding of number. If you would like to read more about the importance of finger work in mathematics, look at the visual mathematics section of youcubed.org. Number lines are really helpful, as they provide the brain with a visual representation of number order. In one study, a mere four 15-minute sessions of students playing with a number line completely eradicated the differences between students from low-income and middle-income backgrounds coming into school (Siegler & Ramani, 2008).

Our brain wants to think visually about mathematics, yet few curriculum materials engage students in visual thinking. Some mathematics books show pictures, but they rarely ever invite students to do their own visualizing and

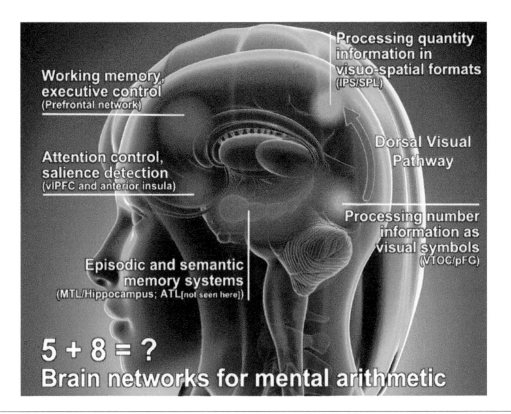

Figure I.5

drawing. The neuroscientists' research shows the importance not only of visual thinking but also of students' connecting different areas of their brains as they work on mathematics. The scientists now know that as children learn and develop, they increase the connections between different parts of the brain, and they particularly develop connections between symbolic and visual representations of numbers. Increased mathematics achievement comes about when students are developing those connections. For so long, our emphasis in mathematics education has been on symbolic representations of numbers, with students developing one area of the brain that is concerned with symbolic number representation. A more productive and engaging approach is to develop all areas of the brain that are involved in mathematical thinking, and visual connections are critical to this development.

In addition to the brain development that occurs when students think visually, we have found that visual activities are really engaging for students. Even students who think they are "not visual learners" (an incorrect idea) become fascinated and think deeply about mathematics that is shown visually—such as the visual representations of the calculation 18 × 5 shown in Figure I.6.

In our Youcubed teaching of summer school to sixth- and seventh-grade students and in our trialing of Youcubed's WIM materials, we have found

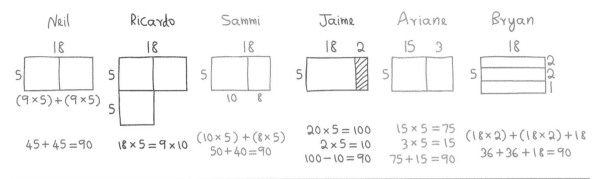

Figure I.6

that students are inspired by the creativity that is possible when mathematics is visual. When we were trialing the materials in a local middle school one day, a parent stopped me and asked what we had been doing. She said that her daughter had always said she hated and couldn't do math, but after working on our tasks, she came home saying she could see a future for herself in mathematics. We had been working on the number visuals that we use throughout these teaching materials, shown in Figure I.7.

The parent reported that when her daughter had seen the creativity possible in mathematics, everything had changed for her. I strongly believe that we can give these insights and inspirations to many more learners with the sort of creative, open mathematics tasks that fill this book.

We have also found that when we present visual activities to students, the status differences that often get in the way of good mathematics teaching disappear. I was visiting a first-grade classroom recently, and the teacher had set up four different stations around the room. In all of them, the students were working on arithmetic. In one, the teacher engaged students in a mini number talk; in another, a teaching assistant worked on an activity with coins; in the third, the students played a board game; and in the fourth, they worked on a number worksheet. In each of the first three stations, the students collaborated and worked really well, but as soon as students went to the worksheet station, conversations changed, and in every group I heard statements like "This is easy," "I've finished," "I can't do this," and "Haven't you finished yet?" These status comments are unfortunate and off-putting for many students. I now try to present mathematical tasks without numbers as often as possible, or I take out the calculation part of a task, as it is the numerical and calculational aspects that often cause students to feel less sure of themselves. This doesn't mean that students cannot have a wonderful and productive relationship with numbers, as we hope to promote in this book, but sometimes the key mathematical idea can be arrived at without any numbers at all.

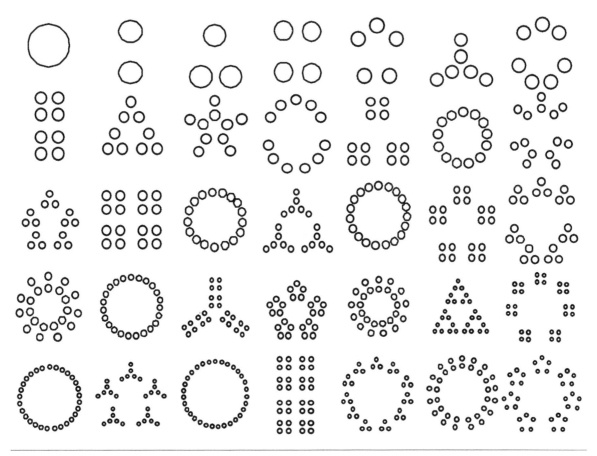

Figure I.7

Almost all the tasks in our book invite students to think visually about mathematics and to connect visual and numerical representations. This encourages important brain connections as well as deep student engagement.

Play

The key to reducing status differences in mathematics classrooms, in my view, comes from *opening* mathematics. When we teach students that we can see or approach any mathematical idea in different ways, they start to respect the different thinking of all students. Opening mathematics involves inviting students to see ideas differently, explore with ideas, and ask their own questions. Students can gain access to the same mathematical ideas and methods through creativity and exploration that they can by being taught methods that they practice. As well as reducing or removing status differences, open mathematics is more engaging for students. This is why we are inviting students, through these mathematics materials, to play with mathematics. Albert Einstein famously once said that "play is the highest form of research." This is because play is an opportunity for ideas to be used and developed in the service of something enjoyable. In the Play activities of our materials, students are invited to work with an important idea in a free space where they can enjoy the freedom of mathematical play. This does not mean that the activities do not teach essential mathematical content and practices—they do, as they invite students to work with the ideas. We have designed the Play activities to downplay competition and instead invite students to work with each other, building understanding together.

Investigate ❓

Our Investigate activities add something very important: they give students opportunities to take ideas to the sky. They also have a playful element, but the difference is that they pose questions that students can explore and take to very high levels. As I mentioned earlier, all of our tasks are designed to be as low floor and high ceiling as possible, as these provide the best conditions for engaging all students, whatever their prior knowledge. Any student can access them, and students can take the ideas to high levels. We should always be open to being surprised by what our learners can do, and always provide all students with opportunities to take work to high levels and to be challenged.

A crucial finding from neuroscience is the importance of students struggling and making mistakes—these are the times when brains grow the most. In one of my meetings with a leading neuroscientist, he stated it very clearly: if students are not struggling, they are not learning. We want to put students into situations where they feel that work is hard, but within their reach. Do not worry if students ask questions that you don't know the answer to; that is a good thing. One of the damaging ideas that teachers and students share in education is that teachers of mathematics know everything. This gives students the idea that mathematics people are those who know a lot and never make mistakes, which is an incorrect and harmful message. It is good to say to your students, "That is a great question that we can all think about" or "I have never thought about that idea; let's investigate it together." It is even good to make mistakes in front of students, as it shows them that mistakes are an important part of mathematical work. As they investigate, they should be going to places you have never thought about—taking ideas in new directions and exploring uncharted territory. Model for students what it means to be a curious mathematics learner, always open to learning new ideas and being challenged yourself.

* * *

We have designed activities to take at least a class period, but some of them could go longer, especially if students ask deep questions or start an investigation into a cool idea. If you can be flexible about students' time on activities, that is ideal, or you may wish to suggest that students continue activities at home. In our teaching of these activities, we have found that students are so excited by the ideas that they take them home to their families and continue working on them, which is wonderful. At all times, celebrate deep thinking over speed, as that is the nature of real mathematical thought. Ask students to come up with creative representations of their ideas; celebrate their drawing, modeling, and any form of creativity. Invite your students into a journey of mathematical curiosity and take that journey with them, walking by their side as they experience the wonder of open, mindset mathematics.

A Note on the Structure of Kindergarten

In the rest of this series, we suggest that teachers delve into a big idea and use the three tasks we provide in order as a framework for a unit of study on that idea. In kindergarten, the rhythm of learning is typically different, and students are often just entering schooling for the first time. At the start of the year, students are actively building stamina for listening to you and one another, for sitting, and for engaging in activity. Partner work on any task is likely new and will require lots of negotiation. Furthermore, students need extended opportunities to engage in activities that are becoming familiar as they develop and refine strategies for counting, grouping, sorting, building, joining, separating, and patterning.

For these reasons, you may want to approach the activities in each big idea somewhat differently. We suggest that the Visualize and Play activities will be useful as you introduce students to new ideas, and students may need lots of opportunities to engage with these or similar tasks over many days or weeks. At the end of each activity, we have provided an extension that discusses how to turn the activity or some part of it into a small-group activity that you can facilitate or a center that students can return to repeatedly with a partner or independently. These extensions amplify what students can learn from each activity by creating venues for ongoing work with the ideas involved.

You may find that it makes sense then to return to the Investigate activities later in the year, once students have more stamina for extended work and greater independence. Many of these activities encourage students to explore ideas, look for patterns, or create a product in ways that they will be better prepared to do by midyear. This structure is more consistent with the ongoing and interconnected nature of the big ideas in kindergarten, which often develop simultaneously or nonlinearly. For instance, counting is not a unit of study but an endeavor that students must engage with consistently as they develop and connect the many ideas involved in asking, "How many?" By making counting and other ideas ongoing explorations and then bringing a rich investigation into class when students are ready, you will support your students in building a solid conceptual foundation for mathematical thinking.

References

Lockhart, P. (2012). *Measurement*. Cambridge, MA: Harvard University Press.

Siegler, R. S., & Ramani, G. B. (2008). Playing linear numerical board games promotes low income children's numerical development. *Developmental Science, 11*(5), 655–661. doi:10.1111/j.1467-7687.2008.00714.x

Thurston, W. (1990). Mathematical education. *Notices of the American Mathematical Society, 37*(7), 844–850.

Note on Materials

Primary classrooms often have a wealth of mathematics manipulatives and materials for modeling and exploring the world. We believe, and extensive research supports, that all math learners benefit from mathematics that is visual, concrete, and modeled in multiple representations. Students need to physically create, draw, and construct mathematics to build deep understanding of what concepts represent and mean. Students need to interact with mathematics, manipulating representations to pose and investigate questions. Apps and digital games are another choice, and we have found them to be valuable because they can be organized and manipulated with an unending supply. However, we want to emphasize that they should not be a replacement for the tactile experience of working with physical manipulatives. We support different tools being available for students to use for representation as they see fit, and afterward we encourage you to ask students to reflect on what the tools allowed them to see mathematically.

Throughout our books, you will find an emphasis on visual mathematics and using manipulatives. The list that follows includes the materials that we use in the lessons in this book, along with how we see these tools as being relevant to mathematics learning. If manipulatives or materials are not available in your building, understanding the purpose of these tools may help you locate substitutes that will support students in engaging with the big ideas in this book.

Manipulatives and Materials Used in This Book

- **Snap cubes.** Snap or linking cubes are perhaps the most flexible mathematical manipulative, and we recommend these for all grade levels. In kindergarten, cubes can be used for counting and organizing, either as loose objects or joined into groups. Linking cubes together, students can see the linear quality of number, and numbers can be composed and decomposed into parts, supporting the concepts of joining and separating.

- **Square tiles.** Square tiles are a flexible manipulative that can be used to represent square units and build patterns from squares physically. In kindergarten, we use these tools, along with blocks, to construct and analyze pyramid patterns, building a foundation for algebraic thinking.

- **Dice.** Dice are used for game play and to explore counting and joining. Dice are wonderful tools for supporting subitizing, or recognizing quantities without counting, which students will learn to do more readily with many opportunities to work with dice.

- **Pattern blocks.** Pattern block sets consist of many copies of six different shapes: square, equilateral triangle, trapezoid, hexagon, and two different parallelograms. These shapes are designed with specific angles to fit together for tiling and such that larger shapes can be decomposed into some of the smaller shapes. In kindergarten, we use pattern blocks to support students in learning to compose larger shapes from smaller shapes.

- **Colors.** Drawing is one entry point for modeling mathematical situations and for recording counting. Drawings can ultimately include labels, such as numbers and words, and can be a starting point for mathematical writing. Later, color-coding work becomes a powerful tool to support decomposition, patterning, and connecting representations. We often ask that students have access to colors; whether they are markers, colored pencils, or colored pens, we leave up to you.

- **Collections of small objects.** Collections of objects offer students of all ages the opportunity to count, organize, sort, and estimate. In most cases, there are many different types of objects that can support this kind of mathematical work, such as beads, coins, bears, pencils, or buttons, in addition to the math manipulatives discussed earlier. In kindergarten, we particularly recommend buttons for one of our sorting activities because buttons have many attributes that can be used to create groups.

- **Tools for organizing, such as bowls, cups, or muffin tins.** As students are developing ideas about how to sort and organize objects for counting or to understand properties, they will benefit from tools that help them maintain organization. Paper cups or bowls work well, as will other small containers or bins. We also like muffin tins for very small objects because they are more difficult to knock over.

- **Digital cameras.** These are optional tools in any activity where they are called for, but when available, digital cameras on any type of device offer kindergar-teners the opportunity to precisely capture their thinking. We use cameras to capture the patterns, constructions, and organization of manipulatives or materials that students create. Students also use cameras to capture patterns and numbers they see in the real world of their classrooms, school, or community.

- **School supplies, such as construction paper, glue sticks, sticky notes, index cards, pipe cleaners, erasers, paper clips, and masking tape.** We use these across the book to construct charts, display thinking, or piece together work. In kindergarten, we use ordinary office or school supplies to support sorting objects, and any mix of available objects will do.

BIG IDEA 1

Understanding the Physical Quantity of Number

The most important goal for any teacher of mathematics, in my view, should be the development of curiosity and wonder in students. When students are curious, they become motivated and inspired to learn anything they set out to learn. There is probably no more important time to spark this journey of curiosity than when students are beginning kindergarten. This becomes particularly important if students are in homes where parents think they should get their children ahead in school by teaching mathematical methods to memorize. If students think their role is to remember inflexible sets of rules, they will be hampered in their mathematical journeys. There is a very strong danger that this approach leads them to believe that this is what math is—a set of rules—that they do not need to make sense of, only memorize. In an international survey given to over 13 million students as part of the international PISA testing, from the OECD, it was found that students who took a memorization approach to mathematics were the lowest-achieving students in every country (Boaler & Zoido, 2016). Unfortunately, the elementary school years are often when students develop the idea, from damaging practices such as timed tests (Boaler, 2014), that mathematics is all about memorization. The opposite of a dry, unappealing, memorization approach to mathematics is one that encourages curiosity and wonder.

We invite students to wonder in all of the activities in this book, starting with Big Idea 1. In the Visualize activity, we ask students to discuss times when they have wondered "How many?" and then give students different groups of objects and invite them to work out how many there are.

In our Play activity, we have chosen photographs for students that include several different things to count, and different ways to count them. We have chosen photographs that offer different ways to count in order to help students know that in mathematics there are usually many different ways to see things and varied ways to approach them, and that different approaches can all be correct if students justify their thinking and give reasons for their approach.

In our Investigate activity, we invite students to make their own books. We recommend that students work in pairs. Each pair is given a number for which to make a page for the class counting book and, if possible, a digital camera. Students can then be taken to spaces where they look for numbers in the world. Together the class makes a whole book that they can refer back to during the rest of the year.

Jo Boaler

References

Boaler, J., & Zoido, P. (2016, November 1). Why math education in the US doesn't add up. *Scientific American.* Retrieved from https://www.scientificamerican.com/article/why-math-education-in-the-u-s-doesn-t-add-up/

Boaler, J. (2014). Fluency without fear: Research evidence on the best ways to learn math facts. Retrieved from http://youcubed.org/teachers/2014/fluency-without-fear/

Count a Collection

Snapshot

Students stretch their counting capacity by counting collections of classroom objects and coming to agreement with a partner about how many objects there are.

Connection to CCSS
K.CC.4, K.CC.5, K.CC.1

Agenda

Activity	Time	Description/Prompt	Materials
Launch	5–10 min	Ask students what kinds of "How many?" questions they have asked themselves. Tell students that they are going to work with a partner to come to agreement about how many objects are in a given group. Model with a partner how to compare counts and resolve any disagreement.	Collection of objects (fewer than 10) in a container
Explore	15–30 min	Partners work together to count a collection of objects and come to agreement about how many there are.	• Collections of various class-room or every-day objects in containers • Optional: sticky notes or index cards
Discuss	10 min	Gather the class in a circle and invite partners to share how they counted their collections. Partners can demonstrate the ways they counted. Highlight features of counting that you'd like to see others try, such as moving objects to count.	Optional: chart and markers
Extend	Ongoing	Create a counting station with a collection of objects for the class to count in small groups or independently over the course of several days. Provide tools for recording the various counts. Discuss how many are in the collection and come to agreement.	• Collection to count • Tools for record-ing, such as sticky notes or index cards

To the Teacher

Counting concepts are at the heart of kindergarten mathematics, and educators who both research mathematics learning and write for teachers have made counting central to considering early mathematics. The notion of repeated, ongoing counting of collections of objects is the subject of two books that we recommend: Franke, Kazemi, and Turrou's (2018) *Choral Counting & Counting Collections* and Liu, Dolk, and Fosnot's (2007) unit of study *Organizing and Collecting*, which is part of the Contexts for Learning curriculum series. Both of these resources provide clear ideas for how to incorporate counting collections of classroom and everyday objects into the long-term trajectory of the early childhood classroom. In this activity, we outline a skeleton of what this work can look like, but the research that Franke et al. have conducted in this area makes clear that counting is less an activity than a routine.

One of the key ideas in counting collections is that the size of the collections can and should be tailored to students' development of counting concepts, such as the oral counting sequence and one-to-one correspondence. When students are getting started, collections will probably need to contain fewer than 10 objects, and for some students perhaps no more than 6. But this number can grow toward and beyond 20 objects as students' counting capacity grows. Indeed, we return to this idea in the final big idea in this book with the premise that students can count toward and beyond 100 objects later in the year. But this growth is only possible with ongoing opportunities to count, recount, and learn to organize objects for counting.

The collections you provide for students to count should be ordinary classroom objects, such as books, cubes, bears, crayons, markers, counters, tiles, or clothespins. Collections should be offered in some kind of container, such as a bag, bowl, bucket, or tray. You'll want to have plenty of collections ready to offer students when they are ready to try a new group of objects. Be sure these collections have a varied number of objects, depending on what your students might be ready for, so that you can direct students toward collections that will stretch their counting capacities.

Activity

Launch

Launch the activity by asking students, Have you ever wondered, "How many?"? Ask students, What kinds of "How many?" questions have you wondered? Give students a chance to turn and talk to a partner about the kinds of situations where they have wondered, "How many?" Listen in as students talk, and revoice some of

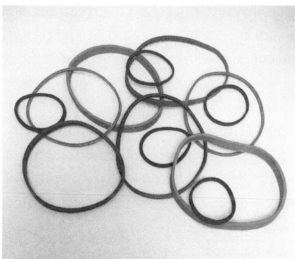

Examples of small collections
for students to count

the questions you hear. You might hear such questions as "How many cookies can I have for dessert?" "How many people are in our class?" "How many stairs are in the staircase?" "How many pets do you have?"

Tell students that asking "How many?" is something that we all do every day. Tell students that today they are going to start figuring out ways to answer those questions by counting groups or collections of objects.

Show students a small group of objects from your classroom. The group should contain more than 5 and fewer than 10 objects. Ask, If my partner and I want to figure out how many there are, what could we do? Model how you and a partner count the group and check with each other by asking, Do we agree? Tell students that they will be working with a partner to count a collection of objects together and that they should come to agreement about how many there are. This might mean counting the group several times until they can agree.

Explore

Provide each partnership with a group of objects to count. Partners work together to count the group of objects and figure out how many there are. Students work to come to agreement about the count, resolving any differences through recounting together.

As you observe students counting, pay attention to *how* they are counting and look for strategies you might want to have them share with the class. You'll also want to attend to opportunities to sit down with students and help them with the number sequence or to resolve disagreements.

Offer students new collections to count as they finish with and agree on the number objects in the group they've been given. Over time, students can learn to label their count with a sticky note or index card. Students can then get a different collection to count and check whether the label attached is correct.

Discuss

Bring students together in a circle to discuss how many objects they found in their collections and how they know. Invite students to share some of their ways of counting. You'll want to select students to share who have useful or new strategies for counting or who resolved a disagreement about the count in a way that others can learn from. When groups share, ask them to put their collection in the center of the circle and show how they counted.

Notice aloud the structures students use to count and organize for counting, such as moving objects as they count them, lining them up, touching each one, or saying the number name as they touch. By highlighting these counting concepts, others will be able to see new ways they might count their collections the next day. You may want to create a class Ways We Count chart to record some of the strategies students find useful.

Extend

As we said in the To the Teacher section, we see this as an ongoing counting routine that can extend for weeks. However, you can also extend this activity by setting up a counting station on a table in your classroom. Have a collection that students can count and recount at the station that might be slightly larger than what they counted in this activity. In small groups, they can visit the station over the course of several days and try to figure out how many objects make up the collection. Over time, students can learn to label their count, and at the end of the week, as a class you can discuss, using the various labels students made, how many there might be. You can create a shared visual proof of how many by asking students to model their counting and to recount until the class can agree. In some ways, this activity works like a number talk stretched across a week.

Look-Fors

- **Are students counting with one-to-one correspondence? Where does one-to-one correspondence break down?** One-to-one correspondence refers to assigning one number name to each object, typically accompanied by touching that object. This requires coordinating the rhythm of the counting sequence with the rhythm of touching the objects, and it reflects an understanding that the numbers refer to the objects being counted. However, one-to-one correspondence isn't something that students have or lack wholesale; students can have one-to-one correspondence up to a point and then have it break down. For instance, you might see students count with one-to-one correspondence through six and then the oral counting sequence begins to go faster or slower than their hands, leading to an inaccurate total count. The more students work to stretch their count a bit beyond their threshold for one-to-one correspondence, the further that threshold will extend. Expect that students will need to count repeatedly and that this is active learning work. Use your observations of students' threshold for one-to-one correspondence to choose collections for them to count that are just beyond what they can comfortably count.

- **Where do students struggle with the counting sequence?** You may see students have one-to-one correspondence, but the number names they assign to each object are not in the conventional order. For instance, students may count a set: "1, 2, 3, 4, 5, 6, 7, 8, 9, 10, 11, 12, 14, 16, 15, 18, 19, 15, 18, 19,..." You may observe gaps in the sequence with skipped numbers, often in the teens; reversals of order; or repetitions. This indicates that students need support with the counting sequence, not the concept of counting. In English, the counting sequence through 12, and to some degree through 20, does not have an internal logic; students simply have to remember these words. Anything that has to do with memory is subject to forgetting. If you see students experiencing difficulties with the counting sequence that create disagreements among partners, you can support them by sitting down to do the counting sequence together, but be sure not to take over the job of touching or moving the objects. We encourage you to incorporate some choral counting routines to support students in learning the oral counting sequence (see Franke et al., 2018).

- **Are students moving objects to track their count?** To keep track of the objects that they have already counted and those that they have not yet counted, it is useful for students to move objects as they count. This is one of the first organizing-to-count ideas that students learn, which in the future can also include lining objects up and grouping objects in 2s, 5s, or 10s. If you notice that students are not moving objects and also struggling to agree on a count, you might ask, Is there a way to keep track of which object you've counted? If you do notice students moving objects to count, point this out and ask, Why did you move the objects like that? Invite these students to share their counting strategy with the class during the discussion to highlight how moving helps us keep track of our counting and come to agreement.

- **How are partners resolving disagreements about how many objects are in their collection?** Conceptually, it is important that students recognize that if two people each count the same collection, they should find the same number of objects. Initially, students are likely to simply accept that one person counted eight and the other counted nine. Pose questions to challenge this acceptance and introduce the need to come to agreement, such as, "So, are there eight bears or nine bears?" You will likely need to prompt students to count again to check in order to support them in learning that recounting is a strategy for resolving disagreements or becoming confident in the count. You may also be able to ask, How could we figure out whether it is eight bears or nine bears? Encourage students who disagree to make their counting clear to each other. You might say things like, "Let's show him how you counted. Why don't we put the bears in the middle here. If you count slowly, we can see how you did it." These kinds of moves encourage precision, recounting, and organizing, while at the same time the observing partner learns to follow someone else's count visually. You can also ask them to count together, both touching and counting aloud so that they can each hear where their counts differ and discuss it. If students cannot come to agreement through recounting, bring the collection to the class during the discussion and invite others to help with resolving the disagreement. You might say to the class, "We cannot figure out whether this group has eight bears or nine bears. Can you help us? What can we do to figure it out together?"

Reflect

How can we count a group of objects so that we know how many there are?

References

Franke, M. L., Kazemi, E., & Turrou, A. C. (2018). *Choral counting & counting collections.* Portsmouth, NH: Stenhouse.

Liu, N., Dolk, M., & Fosnot, C. T. (2007). *Organizing and collecting: The number system.* Portsmouth, NH: Heinemann.

How Many Do You See?

Snapshot

Students use images to answer the question, How many do you see? in multiple ways.

Connection to CCSS
K.CC.5, K.CC.4, K.CC.1, K.CC.3

Agenda

Activity	Time	Description/Prompt	Materials
Launch	5–10 min	Show students the School Supplies image and ask, How many do you see? Students share how many they saw and what objects they focused on. Highlight that there are many things to count in the picture and many ways to count them.	School Supplies sheet, to display
Play	15–20 min	Partners use a new image to explore the question, "How many do you see?" Partners label their counts on the image and try to find many different ways to count what they see. Students can move on to new images when ready.	• How Many Do You See? images, multiple copies per partnership • Tools for labeling
Discuss	10 min	Beginning with the shared image, students show what they counted and how they counted what they saw. Invite students to share the ways they labeled their counts on the image. Highlight language to make clear what is being counted.	How Many Do You See? images, to display

Activity	Time	Description/Prompt	Materials
Extend	Ongoing	Make a station or center with images for students to count with a partner how many they see. Students label their counts on the sheet.	• Images, either from the set provided here or your own • Tools for labeling • Optional: sheet protectors

To the Teacher

In this activity, we build on the work students are doing counting collections, by counting objects in an image. This is more challenging because students cannot move the objects as they count, and touching an image is not the same experience as touching a three-dimensional object. You will likely find that students can readily count fewer objects in an image than they can in a collection. We draw on Christopher Danielson's (2018) *How Many?* which contains rich images, mostly from the kitchen, for students to count.

One key feature of these images and those we have presented here is that there are several different things to count, and ways to count them, embedded in a single photo. This accomplishes a number of things simultaneously. First, the images are flexible, with multiple answers and ways of seeing. Second, students have choices, making it possible for them to count smaller or larger groups. Third, these images encourage students to attend to the unit of their count. That is, "three" isn't enough of an answer for others to understand; we have to know "Three what?" Finally, the best images encourage students to look at the same objects in multiple ways. For some images, students might consider both the parts and the whole, as in a watercolor set with 12 colors in one case. In others, students might see both what is present and what is missing, as with a pencil case that is partially filled.

We have provided some images, and we encourage you to look at those in Danielson's book as well. However, you and your students can make your own images using materials in your classroom or found in your environment. Alternatively, you might find illustrations in favorite picture books that can be used for this activity. When choosing or composing images for this activity, consider the features named in the previous paragraph to make your images flexible and reasonably complex for young children to count in multiple ways.

Activity

Launch

Launch the activity by showing students the School Supplies image on the document camera. Ask, How many do you see? Give students a chance to look and think. Ask students to give a private thumbs-up on their chests when they have something to share, much as they would in a number talk. We encourage plenty of wait time. Ask students to share how many they saw. Students may simply say a number; press them to be clear about the unit by asking questions such as, "Three what?" and having them restate what they saw, naming both the number and the unit. Draw attention to the idea that they can count many different things in this picture, such as paper clips or pencils.

Tell students that today they will be looking at images with a partner and answering the question, How many do you see?

Play

Provide partners a picture from the How Many Do You See? image set. Students use the image to answer the question, How many do you see? Students try to come up with many different things to count and agree on how many there are. Students might label their counts on the image, by circling groups they counted and adding number labels or by writing at the bottom of the sheet the number and word for the objects they counted. To support the later discussion, provide all partnerships with the same first image, but you can give students different images after this if you think they are ready to explore others.

During this work, promote wondering about the images. One way that students might start to look at these images is by first noticing a group of three objects, which is to say that students begin with an answer. But another is to begin with a wonder, such as, How many colors are there? Instead of providing students with your wonders, ask them, What do you wonder about this image? What could you count?

Discuss

Gather students together and show on the document camera the image that everyone counted. Discuss the following questions:

- How many did you see?
- What did you count?

- How did you know how many there were?
- What did you do when you and your partner disagreed?
- How did you record your counting?

As students share, highlight language they use that makes clear what they counted. They may not always have language for what they counted, and this is a prime opportunity to provide words to describe these objects or parts. Invite students to share other images they counted. You might ask, Did anyone count something interesting in another picture? What did you count, and how many were there?

Extend

This activity can be turned into a station or center where you can place a small set of images for students to count together. Partners can discuss an image, pointing out how many they see and what they are counting. You can either provide enough copies for students to work on recording their counts, or place images in sheet protectors so that students can record with dry-erase markers.

Look-Fors

- **Are students specifying what they are counting?** Units are pivotal in this activity, because we cannot take it for granted that we are counting the same things, as we may be when counting collections or in a dot talk. If you notice students only using numbers with one another, you can ask them directly, "Four what?" or you can encourage the partner to ask this question by saying something like, "Ask your partner, 'Four what?'" Listen for students who are describing what they are counting specifically, such as "12 colors in the paint tray," and invite them to share this during the discussion.
- **How are students keeping track of their counts?** In the Visualize activity, we discussed the role of moving and organizing objects to count. But in this activity, movement isn't possible, and students will need other strategies to support them in keeping track. For small quantities, they may need no support; but with larger groups, they may find that marking counted objects with a pencil is useful. Ask questions to help students think about this issue if they seem to be struggling, such as, How can you keep track of which objects you've counted? Be sure to highlight innovative strategies during the discussion.
- **How are students labeling their counts?** Producing numerals, and remembering which numerals match to the number words, is a difficult task on its own.

This activity provides a real context for practicing this work. Although we don't want students to get bogged down in too much handwriting labor, asking students to label even one of their counts will support them in making connections between images of objects, number words, and numerals. Students may also invent interesting ways of labeling with circles, lines, and arrows, which are useful to share with others during the discussion.

Reflect

What makes counting "how many" in a picture different from counting a collection?

Reference

Danielson, C. (2018). *How many?* Portland, ME: Stenhouse.

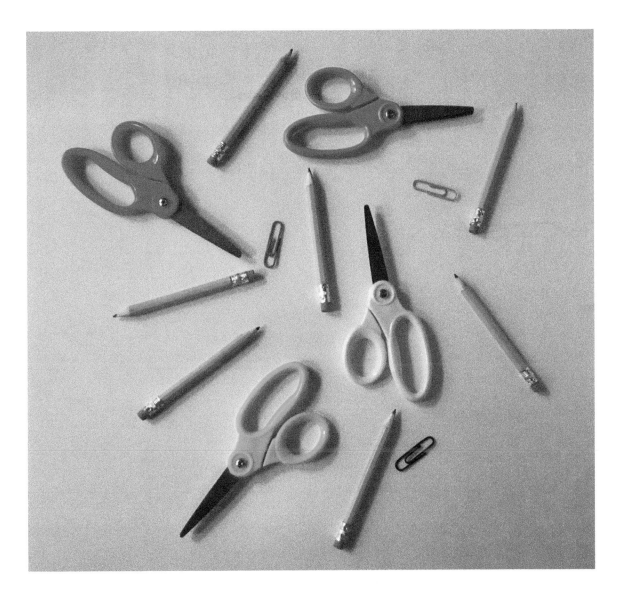

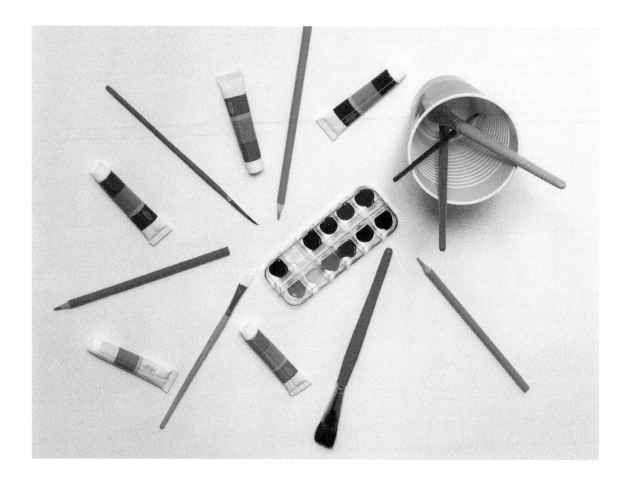

How Many Do You See?

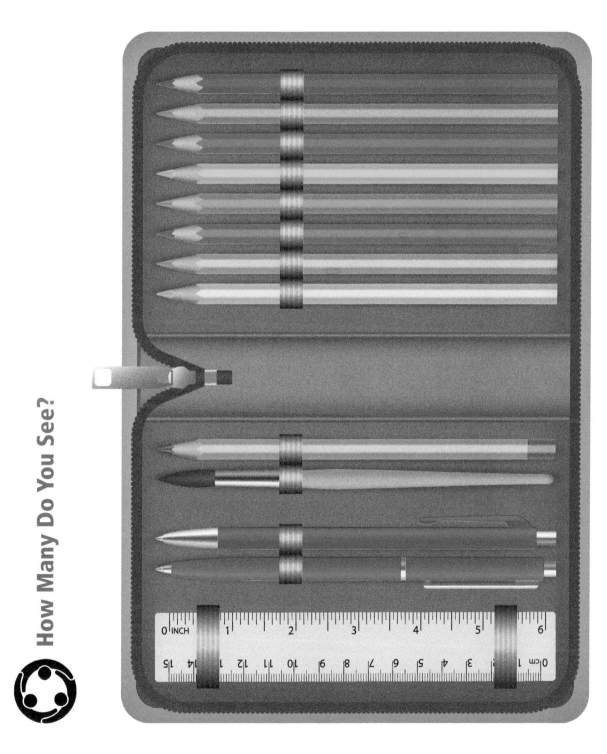

Making a Counting Book

Snapshot

The class works together to construct a counting book using photographs they take of numbers in their world.

Connection to CCSS
K.CC.4, K.CC.5, K.CC.1, K.CC.3, K.CC.6

Agenda

Activity	Time	Description/Prompt	Materials
Launch	10 min	Show students one or more examples of counting books and discuss how the authors show each number. Tell students that they are going to make a class counting book. Decide as a class what features each page should have.	Examples of counting books
Explore	Multiple days	Assign each partnership one or more numbers for which to make a page for the class counting book. Provide partners with a digital camera, if possible, and take students to spaces where they can look for these numbers in the world. Partners then take photos and construct pages for each number they are asked to represent. Construct a class counting book.	• Digital camera, per partnership, or tools for sketching, such as clipboard and colors • Tools for constructing book pages, such as access to computers or construction paper, glue sticks, and colors, depending on the type of book you construct

Activity	Time	Description/Prompt	Materials
Discuss	15 min	Read aloud your class counting book. For each page, ask the class how they see the number represented. Ask the partners who constructed the page how they chose the image to represent the number.	Class counting book
Extend	Ongoing	Make the class counting book available for students to read and take home to share with families. Consider adding pages to the counting book as students extend their counting, particularly for decade numbers.	• Class counting book • Tools for adding to your class book (varies depending on the type of book you constructed)

To the Teacher

In this investigation, we invite students to coconstruct a counting book as a class, an activity inspired by a dear colleague and Pre-K/K teacher, Thora Balk. Counting books are a staple of early childhood, and many excellent examples exist, such as Donald Crews's (1995) *Ten Black Dots*, Lois Ehlert's (1990) *Fish Eyes*, and Zoran Milich's (2007) *City 123*. The most useful counting books, from a math learning perspective, include clear, easy-to-count images in bold colors and with simple shapes. These images are coupled with numerals, and sometimes the number word. It is useful when the number highlights the unit being counted, such as Ehlert's "1 green fish." Milich's book goes one step further, showing the counting sequence all at once with a growing string of dots. We encourage you to read some of these books aloud in advance of launching this investigation so that students are familiar with the genre and can think about the features they might want to include in their own book.

In advance you'll need to decide the range of your class counting book, taking into account how many students you have and the numbers they are comfortable working with. You book could be 1–10, 1–12, 1–20, or go even higher. Students will work in pairs to construct one or more pages for the book, and we encourage you to assign numbers to students mindful of the demands of each number. For instance, it would make sense that the partnership producing the page for number 1 also produce another page, but a partnership making a page for 13 might only make that page.

It is our hope that to construct a page for the book, students can take photographs in the world to represent their number, whether they stage the photos by making a collection of objects in the classroom or go on a number hunt on the playground looking for preexisting groups of objects to represent their number. For instance, in one classroom, we saw students find twigs on the ground with five branches to represent 5 or a set of monkey bars to show 8.

Examples of student photos

The form that your class book takes will depend on your resources and time. You can ask students to physically produce pages, pasting photos on paper and hand-writing labels that can then go in sheet protectors in a binder. You could also scan these physical sheets to print multiple copies of such a book. Or you can use technology to produce a book through a photobook printing service online, or even make a virtual book with slides. However you decide to produce it, consider how you can make the class book available for students to read after it is constructed.

Activity

Launch

Launch the activity by reminding students of all they have been counting with objects and in pictures in the Visualize and Play activities. Show students one or more examples of a counting book, and talk about how these books are organized counting up, with (usually) a page for each number. Show students one page for a particular number, such as 5, and ask, What do the authors put on this page to show 5? Give students a chance to turn and talk, and then take some student ideas. The author may show an image, the numeral, and maybe the number word. Be sure students see that each page follows the same format.

Tell students that they are going to make a counting book as a class, with partners in charge of different numbers. Ask the class, What should we show on each page to help our readers understand the number? Should we have an image? The numeral? The word? Anything else? Come to agreement as a class about what each page should look like. We encourage you to include at least an image and the numeral.

Explore

Assign each partnership one or more numbers for which to make a book page. Provide students with digital cameras. If you don't have access to digital cameras, you can ask students to sketch what they see instead. If you decide on this route, you'll need to provide students with clipboards and colors. Students can capture multiple pictures for their number(s). As a class, you'll need to decide whether students can include multiple pictures on their pages or whether they should choose the clearest or most interesting one for the page.

Take students to places where they are able to look for numbers in the world. This could be your classroom, the school, a playground, a park, or the community. Give students time to explore. They will do a lot of counting, estimating, and comparing in the process.

Once back in the classroom, provide students with access to the materials that match the way you'd like to construct the book, whether those tools are physical (such as construction paper and glue sticks) or digital. Support students in thinking about how to label their images, and remind them of the agreement the class came to about what features they need to include. You may want to support students in constructing their pages in small groups over several days.

Discuss

Read your class book aloud. For each page, ask students to come up and show how they see each number in the images that students created. Ask the creators of each page to share something about how they chose this image or saw it in the world. After you've read your book, ask, What do you think makes our book a helpful counting book?

Extend

Make your class book available in a station or classroom library to be read by students. You could allow students to check it out to take home and share with their families, or read it aloud at a family event at school.

Consider adding on to your book later in the year as students become more comfortable with larger numbers. You could choose to add numbers consecutively (such as 21, 22, 23, 24 . . .) or to highlight only the decade numbers (30, 40, 50, 60 . . .). You could add a page for 100 as a class on the 100th day of school.

Look-Fors

- **Are students thinking expansively about where they might find numbers in their world?** Where students can look for numbers in the world depends on what spaces you take them to for number hunting. However, in every space, some numbers are more obvious, and others are more subtle. For instance, on the playground it may be that students see four swings more readily than a cluster of four acorns on the ground or four points on a poplar leaf. Encourage students to look expansively for examples of their numbers and take many photographs. One of the central goals of this investigation is to promote seeing the world mathematically and noticing numbers everywhere. Even if students quickly find one example of their number, which may be the case for students representing numbers less than 5, challenge them to look for hidden places where they might find their number. This is a good argument for allowing students to include more than one photo on their number page, so both they and the reader can see multiple ways that the number might be represented in the world.

- **As students look for their numbers in the world, are they counting with precision to check?** As students look in the world for their number, they will likely develop hunches about where their number might be found. These hunches are the foundation for estimation. Students might see a stack of books or a branch and think, "That looks about right." It is worth making these hunches explicit and naming them as estimation, as in, "You saw that stack and thought it looked like about six books. You *estimated* it was about six books. That was a useful way of looking for 6." The next step is for students to check their estimates. Valuing the estimate itself means that even when the stack of six books turns out to have five or seven books in it, you can highlight this mathematically useful practice. Encourage students to check their estimates more than once, particularly with items where touching or keeping track of the count may be harder, as with monkey bars high above their heads or the branches on a twig.

- **Are students using any comparative language as they look for their numbers in the world?** Embedded in this counting work are opportunities for students to develop ideas about number comparisons and to connect these to their estimates. When students check the numbers they see in their world, they will likely find times when what they see is more or less than the number they were looking for. In these moments, do you notice students spontaneously using comparative language? Students may use language like *too much, too big, too many, more, less, not enough,* or *too small.* Ask students questions about their reasoning, such as, How do you know? If students simply reject something they counted as not right, press them to make comparisons by asking questions like, How do you know? Or, Is it more or less than your number?

- **Are students attending to the features of a counting book that make numbers clear?** When your class defines the structure of your counting book, students will need to attend to that structure to create a page for the book. They will need to focus on the elements that need to be included and whether there is any format to how they are arranged. This is a form of patterning that we often don't talk about in mathematics, but structured books are patterns. In essence, we are asking students to define and then reproduce the pattern in the form of their pages, and this is far from simple work. Invite students to think about the pattern of the book and the reason for its elements, rather than just telling them what to produce and how. Ask, What parts does your page need? Where do we need to place those parts so that they fit with the other pages in the book? What did we agree on as a class?

Reflect

Where do we see numbers in our world?

References

Crews, D. (1995). *Ten black dots*. New York, NY: Mulberry Books.

Ehlert, L. (1990). *Fish eyes: A book you can count on*. New York, NY: Voyager Books.

Milich, Z. (2007). *City 123*. Toronto, Canada: Kids Can Press.

Using Fingers as Numbers

Sometimes I am really surprised when I read the results of neuroscientific research, and this area of research was one that surprised me more than any other. Research has shown that when we calculate with numbers, an area of our brain lights up that is seeing fingers (Berteletti & Booth, 2015). The harder the mathematics problem, the more likely this brain area is to be activated. It is for this reason that neuroscientists recommend that students spend careful time developing finger perception, which means that students should get to know their different fingers well, through touch. A test for finger perception is to hide one of your hands under a book or table and ask someone to touch your fingertips. People with good finger perception can identify the fingers being touched with ease. A more challenging finger perception test is to touch fingers in two different places—the fingertip and midfinger area.

Here are some interesting facts about finger perception:

- The extent of college students' finger perception predicts their scores on calculation tests (Penner-Wilger & Anderson, 2013).
- Finger perception in first grade is a better predictor of mathematics achievement in second grade than tests (Penner-Wilger et al., 2009).
- Musicians' achievement in higher mathematics, a relationship that has been noted for many years, is now thought to be due to their opportunities for developing good finger perception (Beilock, 2015).

Some teachers and parents believe that finger use in mathematics is babyish and that students should not be allowed to use their fingers. When students of any age are told they cannot use their fingers, we are halting their mathematical development—finger use is that important. For this reason, we have focused this big idea on finger perception, helping students get to know their fingers and know that their fingers are a really important mathematical resource.

In our Visualize activity, students are given opportunities to get to know their fingers by tracing paths through mazes, choosing the right dots to place them on, and playing notes on a "piano." Teachers can choose among these finger perception tasks or have students work on all three of them.

After building finger discrimination in the Visualize activity, we invite students in the Play activity to connect fingers with numbers, using number words and dots on a die. Teachers can play this game with the whole class, rolling a die and asking students to show with their fingers how many dots they see. The class can then come to an agreement together on the number.

In our Investigate activity, partners mirror numbers shown on their hands, and students explore ways to figure out how many fingers are up and down. They can then be invited into discussions of the choices they made.

Jo Boaler

References

Beilock, S. (2015). *How the body knows its mind: The surprising power of the physical environment to influence how you think and feel.* New York, NY: Simon & Schuster.

Berteletti, I., & Booth, J. R. (2015). Perceiving fingers in single-digit arithmetic problems. *Frontiers in Psychology, 6,* 226. doi:10.3389/fpsyg.2015.00226

Penner-Wilger, M., & Anderson, M. L. (2013). The relation between finger gnosis and mathematical ability: Why redeployment of neural circuits best explains the finding. *Frontiers in Psychology, 4,* 877. doi:10.3389/fpsyg.2013.00877

Penner-Wilger, M., Fast, L., LeFevre, J-A., Smith-Chant, B. L., Skwarchuk, S-L., Kamawar, D., & Bisanz, J. (2009). Subitizing, finger gnosis, and the representation of number. *Proceedings of the 31st Annual Cognitive Science Society, 31,* 520–525.

Feeling Fingers

Snapshot

Students build finger discrimination through three activities in which they match their fingers on both hands to colors.

Connection to CCSS
See "To the Teacher"

Agenda

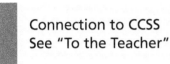

Activity	Time	Description/Prompt	Materials
Launch	10 min	Tell students that their fingers are tools for thinking and give examples of how they already use their fingers to think. Tell students that they are going to do activities to help them know their fingers well. Mark students' fingers with colors. Model one of the three activities.	• Markers for marking students' fingers: red, yellow, green, blue, and purple • Activities sheets for modeling
Explore	15–20 min	Students explore one of three activities: Finger Mazes, Spot On, and Rockin' the Piano.	• Activity 1: make available Finger Maze 1–3 sheets • Activity 2: Spot On sheet, one per student • Activity 3: Rockin' the Piano sheets, cut into strips and taped to a table at seats
Discuss	10 min	Discuss which hand and which fingers it was easier for students to use. Ask students if they felt that it became easier to use their fingers as they worked through the activity(ies) and how they knew.	

Activity	Time	Description/Prompt	Materials
Extend	Ongoing	Students can do all three of these activities as a station or center once they know how each works. Students can create their own versions of each activity using the wireframe or make-your-own templates provided.	• Activity materials set up as a station or center • Optional: Your Own Finger Maze sheets, Spot On Wireframe sheets, and Rockin' the Piano Wireframe sheets and colors for students to customize the activities

To the Teacher

This Visualize lesson is made up of three different smaller activities that you can introduce in succession. Each activity builds finger perception—the ability to discriminate between different fingers and use them independently—starting with Finger Mazes, progressing to Spot On, and then finally Rockin' the Piano. These three activities are adapted from the research of Gracia-Bafalluy and Noël (2008), which found that finger-training exercises like these can support students in learning to perceive their fingers, which in turn supports the learning of mathematics more broadly. Although these kinds of activities, which are precursors to using fingers to represent, compose, and decompose numbers, are not represented among the Common Core State Standards for kindergarten, the research is clear that students' mathematical learning benefits from working with fingers in the absence of numbers.

For these three activities, we recommend that you introduce them one at a time either as parts of the same day of mathematics learning or across three different days. Each activity can then become something that students do in stations or centers either independently or with a partner. To mark students' fingers with color, we recommend using markers on students' fingernails; dot stickers can work, but often fall off. A small color dot with a marker is quick and won't disappear during the activity.

Activity

Launch

Launch the activity by telling students that fingers are tools for thinking. Knowing your fingers well helps you think. Give students some examples of how they use their fingers to think, such as using them to show how old we are, counting, and moving our hands when we talk.

Tell students that they are going to work on three different activities that help them get to know their fingers well. Show students that they are going to mark their fingers with colors so that we all have a way of talking about each finger as a color. Mark each finger with a single color: yellow for thumbs, red for index fingers, green for middle fingers, blue for ring fingers, and purple for pinkies. You can change the order of these colors later to continue to use the activities and keep them challenging.

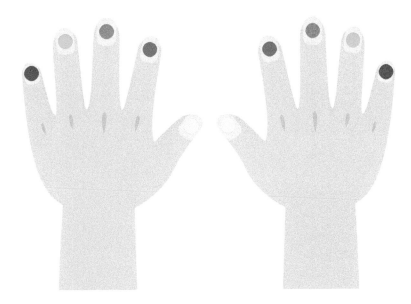

Hands with each finger of the left hand identified with a different colored dot on the fingernail. The right-hand colors are a mirror image of the left.

Source: Shutterstock.com/logistock.

Show students one of the activities and how they will match their fingers by color and touch or trace. Have a student model how to do this for the group.

Explore

Activity 1: Finger Mazes

Provide students with access to the three Finger Maze sheets. Students can play this independently and do not need to mark on the sheet. Sheets can be swapped for new mazes and reused by others.

Students match a finger to the line with the same color, and trace from the start to the end. They can do this with each hand and each color. Students can do the same maze repeatedly, and move through all three mazes.

Activity 2: Spot On

Provide each student with the Spot On sheet. This activity can be played as a small or whole group. In this game, the teacher calls out two colors, one for each hand. Students will then match a finger on each hand to any dot of the same color on the board. If you want to encourage students to learn left and right, you can call these colors out as, for example, "Left hand, blue. Right hand, yellow." Otherwise you can simply say, "With one hand, match to blue. With the other hand, match to yellow." Students would then find the blue finger on one hand and place it on any blue dot, and find the yellow finger on the other hand and match it to any yellow dot. This takes time for students to figure out; do not rush them. Repeat calling out several different color combinations. Students can later play this in partners or small groups by taking turns calling colors for each other.

Activity 3: Rockin' the Piano

Prepare a space as a piano station for a small group by cutting the Rockin' the Piano sheets into strips so that each one can be taped to a separate table surface for a child to sit at. Each of these strips creates a different piano. We've included a blank if you (or students) would like to design your own.

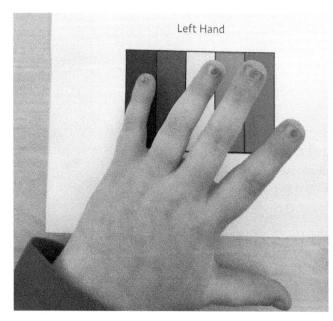

The left-hand pinky finger, with a purple dot on the fingernail, is placed on the Left Hand purple key.

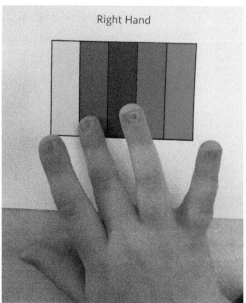

The right-hand middle finger, with a green dot on the fingernail, is placed on the Right Hand green key.

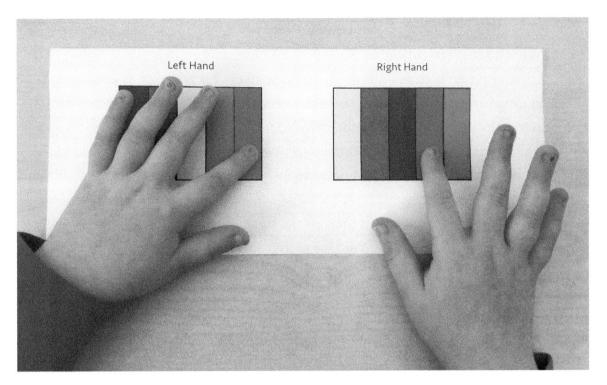

A child plays the red key for the left and right hands simultaneously.

Students can play this game independently. Sitting at one of the pianos, each student plays the keys in order for each hand. Once students feel comfortable with single-hand play, they can move on to using both hands. Starting on the left (or right) of each group of keys, students play each key on both hands simultaneously. After students have a chance to play one piano a few times, they can rotate to a new piano.

Discuss

After students have had a chance to do one or more of these activities, discuss the following questions as a class:

- Was there one hand that was easier to use than the other? Which one?
- Were some fingers easier to use than others? Which ones?
- Did it get easier to match your fingers to the colors? How could you tell?

Extend

All three of these activities can become stations or small-group activities for students to continue to work on over time. We have provided blank templates for each game so that students can create their own versions.

- **Are students attending to the colors?** These activities are intentionally demanding of students' attention to color across both hands. It can be challenging for students to track the color on their hands and then match it to the sheet, placing each finger in the matching location. We start with the finger mazes because these allow students to focus first on just one hand and then the other, rather than both simultaneously. As students move to the Spot On game, they need to hear the color word, imagine what the color word means, match it to their hands, and then to the sheet. This is quite a long chain of connections to follow, and we expect that students will need a lot of time to do so. Providing wait time, repeating colors aloud, and asking specific scaffolded questions (such as, Which finger is blue?) will support students in building the very connections between brain and hands that will help them with mathematical thinking in the long run.

- **Are students tracking and trying both hands?** You are very likely to notice that students are far more fluent when you ask them to work with one hand than with both, and that students' dominant hands are much easier for them to use in any game. Students may even tend to just look at or use one hand, even when the game asks them to use both. Encourage students to use both hands, but to use them one at a time. They may want to first use their dominant hand to, for example, touch a piano key and then, holding that hand down, try to locate the finger they need on their nondominant hand. Keep in mind that students are building neural connections as they do this work, and more time and less pressure will keep this work fun rather than stressful.

Reflect

What did you notice about using your fingers that hadn't noticed before?

Reference

Gracia-Bafalluy, M., & Noël, M. P. (2008). Does finger training increase young children's numerical performance? *Cortex, 44*, 368–375.

Finger Maze 1

Finger Maze 3

End

Finger Maze 4

Start

 **Spot On**

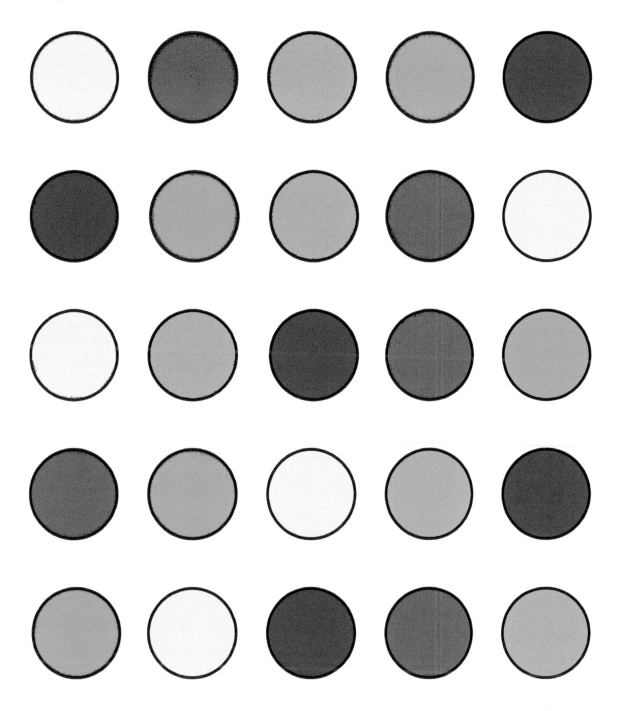

Spot On Wireframe

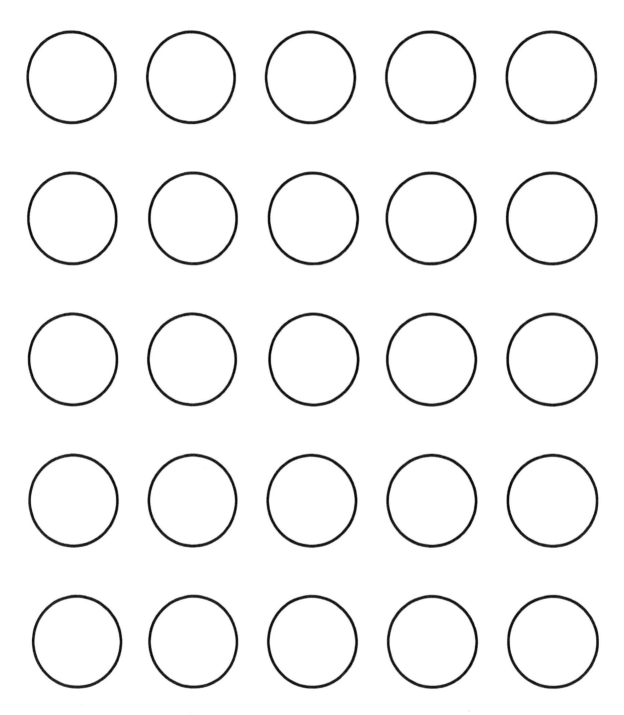

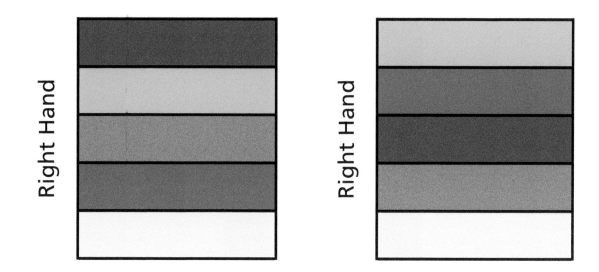

Rockin' the Piano 1

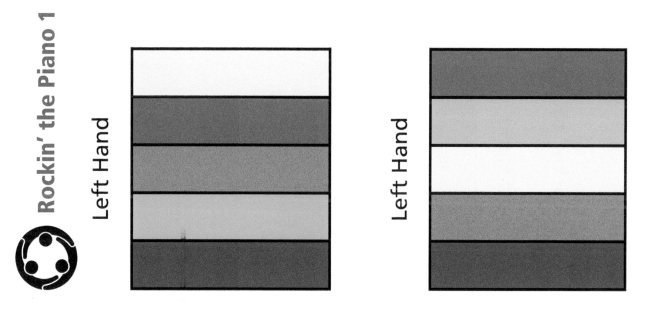

Rockin' the Piano 2

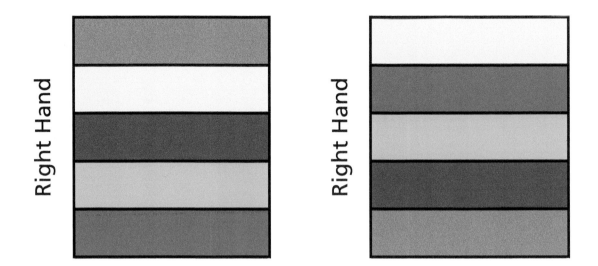

Right Hand

Right Hand

Left Hand

Left Hand

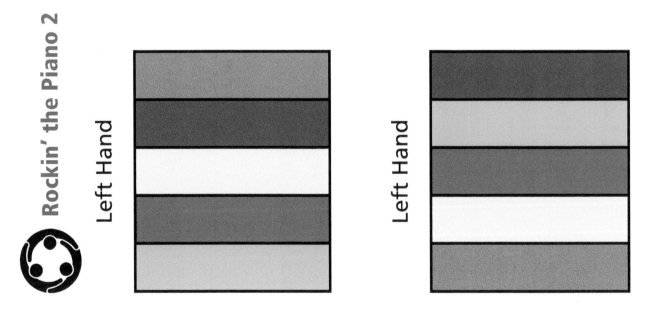

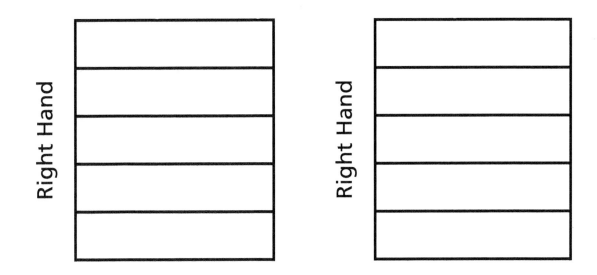

Rockin' the Piano Wireframe

Right Hand

Right Hand

Left Hand

Left Hand

Show Me with Your Fingers

Snapshot

Students show with their fingers the number rolled on a die and try to come up with creative ways to show each number, building both counting and equivalence concepts.

Connection to CCSS
K.CC.4, K.CC.5, K.OA.3

Agenda

Activity	Time	Description/Prompt	Materials
Launch	10–15 min	Play the game Show Me with Your Fingers as a class by rolling a die and asking students to show with their fingers how many dots they see. Come to agreement about how many there are and share different ways to show that number on hands.	Die
Play and Discuss	15–20 min	Play the game Show Me with Your Fingers as a small-group activity with the teacher facilitating. Roll the die and discuss the ways students find to show the number with their fingers. Discuss which numbers were more challenging or interesting to make with their hands, and what interesting ways they saw to show numbers.	Die
Extend	20+ min	Partners play Show Me with Your Fingers, taking turns rolling and showing the number with their fingers. The partner not showing the number then records the dots shown on the die and the way it was shown on hands. Post these recording sheets for students to see the diversity of ways they found to represent numbers with their fingers.	• Die • Show Me with Your Fingers sheets • Colors, per partnership

To the Teacher

Students built finger discrimination in the Visualize activity, and in this activity, we connect fingers with numbers, using both the dots on a die and number words. For this activity, you will be rolling a die so that students can see it. This can be done with a die on a document camera, or you can make a large die out of a foam cube and draw dots on it. We've even seen some very large dice available, some of which are inflatable. A large die or projector will make it easier for everyone to see.

We've structured this activity so that it is first played as a whole class to establish the routine and show students that you value multiple and creative ways of showing numbers on their fingers. Then play the game as a small-group activity that you facilitate. Finally, we transform the game into a partner activity that incorporates recording different ways to show numbers on fingers.

Activity

Launch

Launch the activity by playing the Show Me with Your Fingers game as a whole group. Roll the die so that everyone can see the result clearly. Ask students to show on their hands the number of fingers that is the same as the number of dots they see. Give students a moment to get their hands ready in their laps, then ask them to hold their hands in the air.

Look around to notice the diversity of answers and the ways that students are showing the number with their fingers. For instance, if you roll a 6, you might see students holding up four, five, or six fingers. You will also probably see different ways of showing six fingers, such as five and one or three and three.

Invite students to explain why their fingers match the number of dots on the die. Students may want to come up to the die to show how their fingers match. Come to agreement as a class about how many fingers match the dots on the die, and name this number.

Point out different ways students show the same number on their hands. Ask, Is there another way we can show this number of dots on your fingers? Draw attention to different, but equivalent, presentations of the number with fingers.

Play and Discuss

Play this game as a small-group activity, with you facilitating. After you roll the die, students each make the number of dots with their hands. Ask each student to explain, How do you know your fingers match the dots? If students need to revise

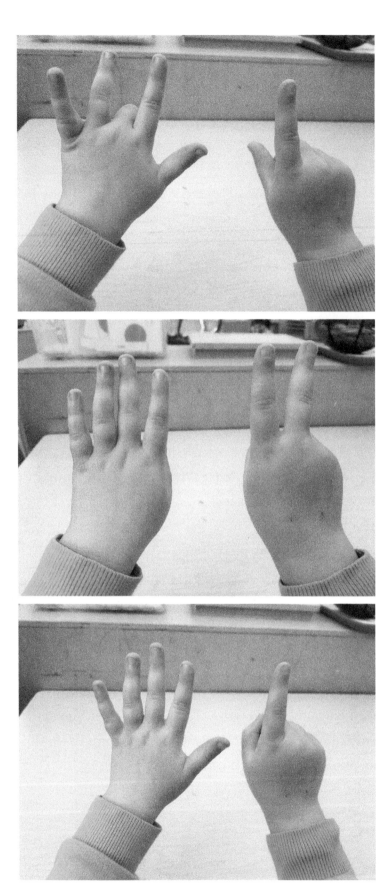

A child shows three different ways to make 6.

their hands as they explain, this is a great opportunity for using mistakes as a site for learning. You can ask, Do you want to revise your answer (or hands)?

During your discussion of each round, draw students' attention to different ways they showed the same number. Challenge students to come up with creative or new ways of showing the number on the die. Students can decompose a number across two hands in different ways or simply use different fingers on the same hand.

Close the small group by discussing the following questions:

- Which numbers were harder to show with your hands? Why?
- Which numbers were more interesting to make? Why?
- What interesting ways to make a number did you see others try today?

Extend

This game can be transformed into a partner game that incorporates recording the number in multiple ways. Provide partners with a die, Show Me with Your Fingers sheets, and colors. Partners play this new version of the game using the following routine:

- Partner A rolls the die. Partner A shows the number of dots with their fingers and explains to Partner B why they match.
- Partner B then colors in the fingers on the Show Me with Your Fingers sheet to match what Partner A is showing. Partner B colors in the die box in the margin to match the dots shown on the die. They can also add the numeral to their recording.
- Partners swap roles and repeat.

Collect students' recordings from playing the game, and post these as different ways to make numbers with our fingers. You can post these sheets whole, or cut apart the sheets and group all the 1s, 2s, 3s, 4s, 5s, and 6s together into separate displays. If you display students' work in this way, you can lead a discussion about what students notice about the ways they found to show each of the different numbers. Students may notice, for instance, that there were fewer ways to show 1 than to show larger numbers.

Look-Fors

- **Are students recognizing or counting the dots on the die?** The structure of the die is powerful for learning to subitize, or recognize small quantities without counting. The die's consistent structure, which utilizes the diagonal, the square, and arrays, can support students in learning to recognize numbers, such as 5 and 6, that in other arrangements would need to be counted one by one. Provide everyone a chance to think, and discourage students from calling out the number. But as you observe students playing this game, pay attention to which students already recognize the number of dots on a die's face, and who needs to count. Those students who need to count the dots simply need more opportunities to work with dice, in this game or others, to build the recognition that will help them in the future.

- **Are students accurately connecting the number of dots to the number of fingers?** With the smaller numbers on the die, students will likely be able to readily represent the dots as fingers. However, with 4, 5, or 6, students may miscount either the dots on the die or the fingers on their hands. If you notice that this is a recurring challenge, build in a moment in the game routine for students to check. You might say, "Look at the dots on the die. Think about how many you see. Now look at your hands. Do you see the same number? You can revise if you notice they don't match."

- **Are students representing numbers on their hands in ways other than those we typically see?** Cultures have canonical ways of representing each number with fingers, and cultures differ with how they do so. You will certainly see students using typical ways of representing each number on their fingers. Without discouraging these ways, encourage diversity. Seeing multiple ways of representing numbers builds flexibility and ideas of equivalence. For instance, when students see 4 represented as four fingers on one hand, and then as two fingers on each hand, and also as three fingers on one hand and one finger on the other, they are building the foundation for understanding why $4 = 2 + 2 = 3 + 1$.

Reflect

What are the most interesting ways you found or saw to make a number with your fingers?

 **Show Me with Your Fingers**

Hand Mirrors

Snapshot

Partners mirror numbers shown on their hands, and students explore ways to figure out how many fingers are up and down.

Connection to CCSS
K.CC.4, K.CC.5, K.OA.4, K.OA.1, K.CC.6

Agenda

Activity	Time	Description/Prompt	Materials
Launch	10 min	Model how to play Hand Mirrors so that students understand the role each partner plays. Tell students that as they play, they should focus on figuring out how to mirror their partner's hands and how many fingers are up and down.	
Explore	15+ min	Partners play Hand Mirrors, with one partner showing a number on their hands and the other mirroring that display. Then they discuss how many fingers are up, how many are down, and how they know.	
Discuss	10 min	Discuss students' strategies for mirroring their partner's hands and for figuring out how many fingers are up and down. Draw attention to ideas that focus on the total number of fingers on one or both hands.	Chart and markers
Extend	30+ min	Partners play Hand Mirrors and record their hands and the number of fingers up and down for each round. Discuss how you might sort the solutions into some groups by asking, How are some of these alike? How are they different? Make some groups and display those solutions that fit into your groups. Discuss which groups have more solutions and which have fewer.	• Hand Mirrors sheets cut into individual recording strips, multiple per partnership • Colors • Space to display solutions

To the Teacher

This investigation activity begins as a game that students can play in partners with their hands. In the game, students use their hands to show numbers, which their partners try to mirror. Mirroring means that students have to attend carefully to how many fingers their partners are showing and how many are folded down. Students then discuss how many fingers are up and how many are folded down, which they may reason about either through counting or by thinking of decomposing the total number of fingers. Students might attend to each hand individually as five fingers, some of which are up and some of which are down, or to their hands together as 10 fingers, doing the same decomposing work. This lays a foundation for decomposing numbers generally and 10 specifically, which we will return to in Big Idea 4.

We extend the game into a larger investigation through the extension. Once students are comfortable with the routine of the game, you can add in recording, using our Hand Mirror sheet, the various ways they are showing numbers on their hands. These can then be sorted as a class to look for similar hand mirrors. This sorting process might focus on numerical similarities, such as different ways to show seven fingers up and three fingers down, or properties of the solutions, such as solutions where the down fingers are on only one hand.

Activity

Launch

Launch the activity by telling students that they are going to play a counting game with their hands. Using a fishbowl discussion, model how to play Hand Mirrors, with you as Partner A and a student as Partner B. Focus students' attention on the process of playing this game so that they know what role each partner plays.

Tell students that as they play, you want them to focus on figuring out how to make their hands look like their partner's and figuring out how they know how many fingers are up and how many are down.

Explore

Partners explore the following Hand Mirrors routine:

- Partner A holds up their hands, with some fingers folded down, so that any folded fingers are facing them and not their partner.

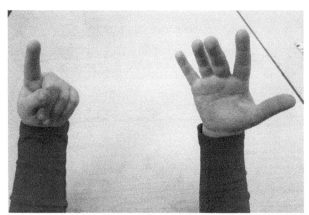 

Partner A shows 6.   Partner B mirrors 6.

- Partner A asks Partner B: Can you make your hands look like mine? Partner A gives Partner B time to try to mirror their hands.
- Partners work together to check that their hands match.
- Partners discuss the following questions:
  - How many fingers are up?
  - How many fingers are down?
  - How do we know?
- Partners swap roles.

As you circulate observing students, press students to talk about how they know how many fingers are up and how many are down.

Discuss

Gather students together to discuss the following questions:

- What was hard about playing Hand Mirrors?
- What strategies did you develop for matching your hands to your partner's?
- How did you know how many fingers were up?
- How did you know how many fingers were down?
- What did you notice about your hands that helped you?

As students discuss strategies, record their thinking on a chart so that others can see how they matched hands or counted fingers. Draw attention to strategies for finding how many fingers are up and down that use the total number of fingers on one or both hands, as these strategies utilize decomposing 5 or 10.

Extend

Partners play Hand Mirrors, and, for each round, they work together to record the way fingers were shown on their hands using sections of the Hand Mirrors sheet, building connections to decomposing 10. Students can mark the up fingers and down fingers using different colors or by crossing out the down fingers. Students then label the number of up fingers and down fingers in the margin.

After students have generated a number of these recordings, gather students as a whole or in small groups to discuss the following questions:

- How are some of these alike?
- What makes them different?
- What groups can we make?

Develop some groups and create a labeled space in which to display those solutions that can be grouped together. These groups might be based on numbers (such as how many fingers are up or down) or properties (such as having a full hand of fingers showing or solutions where the thumbs are both down), and either way is appropriate. Sorting is an idea we will return to in Big Idea 6, and this activity might provide some insight into how students already see shared features. After you sort the solutions, you might discuss which groups have lots of examples in them and which have few.

Look-Fors

- **Are students mirroring hands?** Just the act of mirroring another person's hands is challenging for students in kindergarten. It will likely take students time to look at their partner's hands, try to show it on their own hands, check, and adjust. Be sure partners are being patient with this process and that they are taking the time to check that their hands do match. How do they check? They may simply hold their hands against each other to see if the fingers up and down align, or they may describe something about their hands as evidence that they do not match, such as, "No, your thumb should be up." If students disagree, ask, How could you explain to your partner what they need to do to make their hands look like yours?
- **How are students counting the up and down fingers?** Counting on your fingers when your fingers are occupied can be particularly challenging. In this game, students need to hold some fingers up and down, and both hands are

engaged in the game, leaving them fewer options for how to count. Students may use an up finger from either hand to count the fingers on the opposite hand, though this is tricky work. They may begin to use subitizing to simply see one, two, or three fingers as up or down on each hand. They may track their counting visually by looking at each finger in turn as they count. Observe students as they count and ask them questions about how they counted when their fingers were harder to use.

- **Do students decompose 5 or 10?** You might see some students using the 5 and 10 structure of their hands to figure out how many fingers are up or down. Alternatively, some students might count their fingers in some way, but use 5 or 10 as a check on whether their count makes sense. Ask questions about how students know how many fingers are up or down, and notice instances where students use language like, "Well, I know there are five fingers on my hand . . ." Ask, How does that help you? Be sure to invite these students to share during the discussion so that others might use 5 or 10 as a tool in this game in the future.

Reflect

How could you figure out how many fingers are down when you look at your partner's hands?

Hand Mirrors

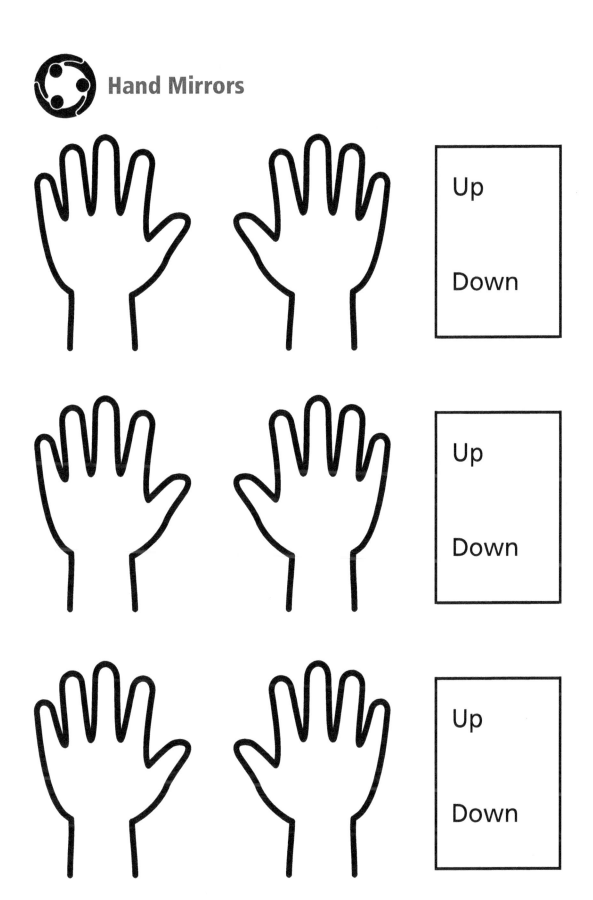

Talking about and Making Shapes

In this set of activities, we invite students to be playful with shapes. Children are naturally curious about shapes in the world, and they only become less curious when the teaching of shape in schools is reduced to lists of attributes, definitions, and names. There is a famous shape-building activity that I have enjoyed introducing to students, called the Marshmallow Challenge. In this activity, teams of students are given 1 marshmallow, 1 yard of string, and 1 yard of tape and asked to build the tallest freestanding structure they can, in a short time, with the marshmallow supported on the top. There is a TED Talk about this activity, featuring author Tom Wujec. He explains that when the task was given to three groups—lawyers, business school graduate students, and kindergarten students—the people with the most success, who built the best and tallest structures, were the kindergarten students. The reason they were more successful is that they experimented freely, whereas the other groups planned carefully without experimenting and trying things out. I love this result, as it shows the free and creative thinking of young students. In this set of three activities, we nurture this free thinking as students work with shapes and think about their qualities.

In our Visualize activity, we invite student to talk about shapes, and gather together the features they describe in the shapes. Students may describe the whole shape and its overall essence, or they may focus in on the components of the shapes, noticing the ways the shapes are constructed.

In our Play activity, we bring in some mystery by giving students some information about a shape you have made and asking them what they think it might be. This activity is the converse of the Visualize activity, where students were asked to describe shapes. In this activity, we give some information and ask students to imagine what the shape might be.

In our Investigate activity, students are given important opportunities to touch and feel shapes, which will stimulate different brain pathways. In this activity, students work with pattern blocks and their imaginations, making any shapes that they want to. We suggest that you show them a turtle made of blocks so that they see the idea of making animals or whatever else they think about. Make a chart of all the different ideas students come up with.

Jo Boaler

Talking about Shapes

Snapshot

Students work together to develop increasingly precise descriptions of two- and, later, three-dimensional figures.

Connection to CCSS
K.G.4, K.G.2

Agenda

Activity	Time	Description/Prompt	Materials
Launch and Explore	15 min	Looking at one Shape Talk figure, invite students to describe what they notice about the shape. Annotate the shape with student descriptions and support students in finding language to describe what they notice. Name the shape and label it. Discuss why this name makes sense or how it is like other shapes with the same name.	• Shape Talk sheet, to display, taped to a chart • Markers
Discuss	5 min	Discuss the words the class used to describe the shape. Underline or record on a chart useful words for describing shapes, such as *sides* or *corners*.	Chart and markers
Extend	15 min	Using the same routine, invite students to explore and describe a three-dimensional figure. Record students' descriptions on a chart. Discuss words that the class can use to describe three-dimensional figures that are the same and different from those they used with two-dimensional shapes.	• Three-dimensional figures, to display • Chart and markers

To the Teacher

This activity is based on work that Rebecca Ambrose (2002; Ambrose & Kenehan, 2009) has been doing for many years exploring how to support students in moving from holistic descriptions of geometric figures, which focus on describing the overall visual appearance (Van Hiele Level 1), toward analytic descriptions, which focus on the components of shapes (Van Hiele Level 2). Ambrose's research has focused on third graders working with polyhedral, three-dimensional figures composed of polygons. Ambrose and Kenehan (2009) found that by providing students with repeated opportunities across the school year to describe and build these figures, students increasingly focused on the components of the figures (e.g., "It is made up of a cube and pyramid") rather than the whole (e.g., "It's a drum"). Building on this research, we have designed this activity, which is a geometry routine, to provide opportunities for kindergarteners to collectively describe two-dimensional figures, with the long-term goal of focusing increasingly on their components.

This is an activity that you can do repeatedly, either in small groups or as a whole group, depending on your students' stamina for discussion. We see this routine as similar to dot or number talks that can be repeated regularly as part of math time over a long period, helping students develop language for shapes and learning what features to pay attention to. Eventually these conversations can lead students to understand what attributes define particular shapes. Given that these are yearlong goals, it is not critical that in any particular shape talk students see all the components of the figure or use formal language. We encourage you to support students in using the language they are ready for, and to add any new words in parallel with students' own language. We have provided some shapes to launch this routine, but you can make your own to continue this work across a unit or the year.

Activity

Launch and Explore

Launch the activity by showing students the triangle on the Shape Talk sheet, which you have printed out and taped to a chart. Tell students that they are going to work together to describe this shape, so that they could tell someone who couldn't see it what it looks like. Ask students, What do you notice about this shape? How could you describe it? Give students a chance to turn and talk to a partner about the shape. Invite students to share ideas.

Facilitate the discussion of the shape by recording students' ideas about the shape on the chart. Use arrows to point to the features students are describing, such as "It has corners." Invite others to add on to the description. Offer students language for attributes where they struggle to find words to describe particular features. Students can come up to the shape to point out what they want to describe, and the class can offer ideas for words they could use. You might ask, How could we describe what they have just pointed out?

Students may also notice holistic features, such as "It's big" or "It's pointy," which represents a beginning point for attending to geometric figures. Students may notice components, such as that the shape has three sides or three corners, that two sides are the same, that one side is shorter, and so on. Honor students' use of gesture to describe the shape. They may not have any words to describe features such as the angles (or, later, parallel lines), and gestures are key resources.

After the class has exhausted its observations, tell students that this shape has a name, *triangle*, if it has not yet been named. Record this word at the top of your description chart. You might say that *tri* means three, as for a tricycle, which has three wheels. Ask, Why might this shape be called "triangle"? Students might notice that the shape has three sides or three corners.

Repeat with other shapes from the Shape Talk sheet set on other days. When students have had experience with multiple examples of the same shape (such as different triangles or different rectangles), put these charts side by side and ask, What makes both of these shapes triangles (or rectangles)? Discuss what the shapes have in common that might make them part of the same group of shapes.

Discuss

Discuss the following questions:

- What words did we use to describe shapes today?
- What kinds of things in a shape did we pay attention to?

Underline key words on your chart that help describe shapes (such as *sides, corners, length/long*). You might start a Words We Use to Describe Shapes chart that can serve as a resource on future days when you do this activity.

Extend

This same activity structure can be used to explore three-dimensional figures, such as cylinders, cubes, or rectangular prisms. You will need objects to display, not drawings of three-dimensional figures, which are too visually challenging to interpret. You can use wooden blocks, a geometric figure set, or everyday objects. You can even construct your own figures with geometric building sets that have pieces that snap together. Be sure to give students opportunities to touch and explore the object from all sides. If you have multiple examples of the figure, you can distribute these to pairs of students to explore. Invite students to describe these objects and record their language on a chart.

Discuss what words they used to describe flat (two-dimensional) shapes that they can also use for these objects, and what new words students might need. For instance, the word *side* may need a new meaning or may need to be replaced when talking about three-dimensional objects, because it is not clear whether *side* means the same thing as *edge* or *face*. Students do not need formal language, but they do need to be able to communicate with one another clearly. Your class will need to agree on the ways they want to use particular terms.

Look-Fors

- **Are students attending to components of the shape, rather than the whole?** Look for student descriptions that focus on particular parts of the shape being discussed, such as the number, position, or length of sides, or the number of corners. Draw attention to these contributions by saying things like, "You noticed that this shape has some parts." Over time, the goal of this activity is for students to pay increasing attention to the parts of shapes, which will help them see how shapes are composed and later to compare those shapes.

- **What words are students using to mean the same thing?** You may hear multiple terms being used to indicate the same thing. Be sure to capture all the different ways that students describe the shape, even if students are simply renaming a feature or description that another student has made. As you do so, make connections between similar descriptors. This can sound like, "You see these as three corners, just like they saw them as three points." You can also record these equivalent descriptions in the same physical space on your chart to show that these are two different ways of describing the same thing. In this way, children build greater fluency with the many ways we describe shapes, while understanding that some words are synonymous.

- **What words do students need to help them describe a feature?** Although it is not important that students use formal language, such as *vertex*, to describe shapes, at times students will have no words to describe what they notice. Invite students to use gestures or to come up and point to the shape to communicate what they notice. Then you can ask the class, How could we describe what they just pointed out? Or you can provide a name for this feature yourself. In either case, you are facilitating pooling the class's vocabulary to provide ways of naming and describing features of geometric figures, broadening the resources of your classroom community.

Reflect

When you see a new shape, what do you pay attention to? Why?

References

Ambrose, R. (2002). Developing spatial understanding through building polyhedrons. *Teaching Children Mathematics, 8,* 442–447.

Ambrose, R., & Kenehan, G. (2009). Children's evolving understanding of polyhedra in the classroom. *Mathematical Thinking and Learning, 11*(3), 158–176. doi:10.1080/10986060903016484

BIG IDEA 3: TALKING ABOUT AND MAKING SHAPES

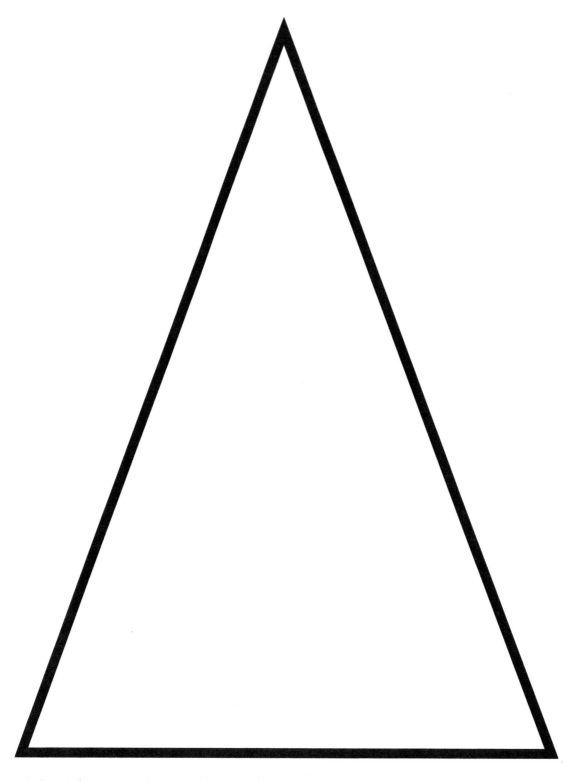

Shape Talk

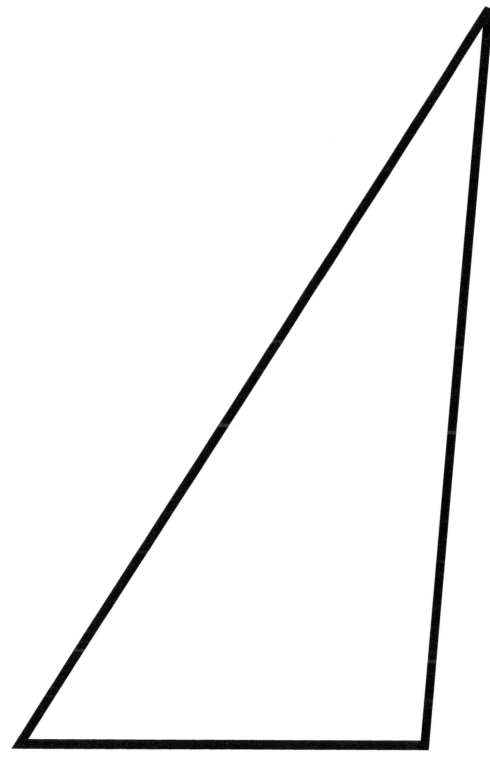

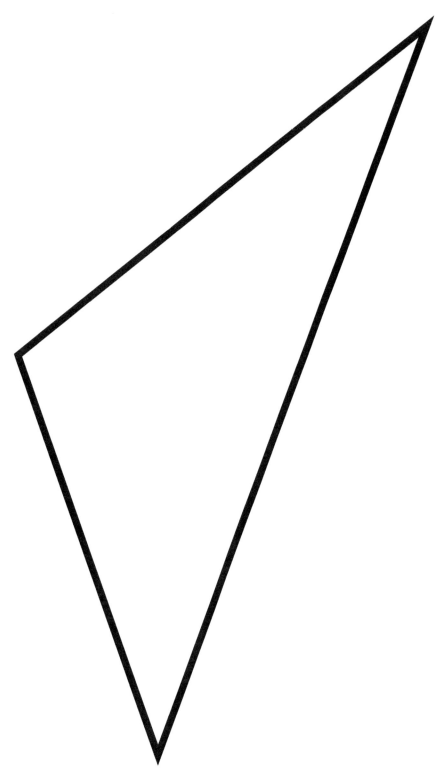

 **Shape Talk**

Shape Talk

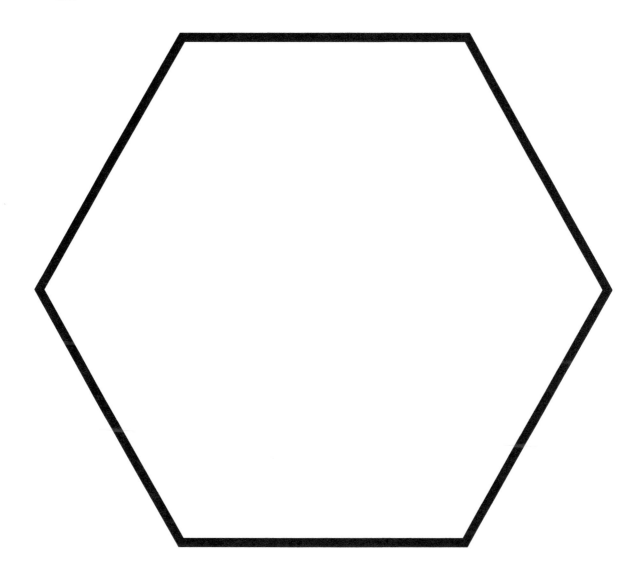

 **Shape Talk**

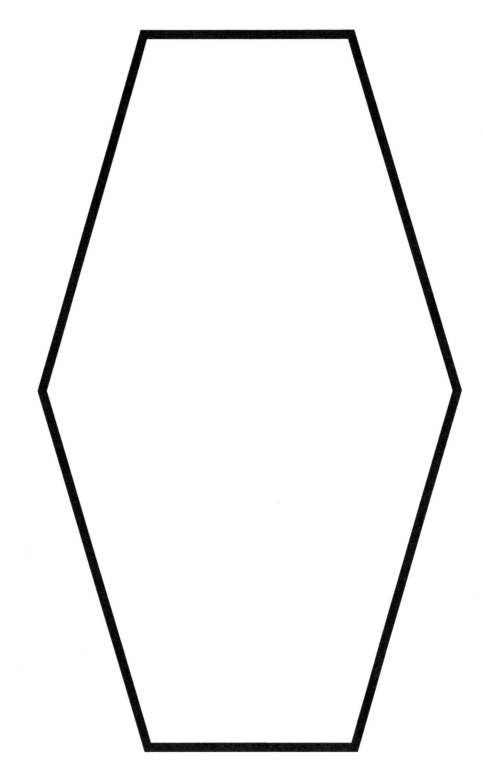

 **Shape Talk**

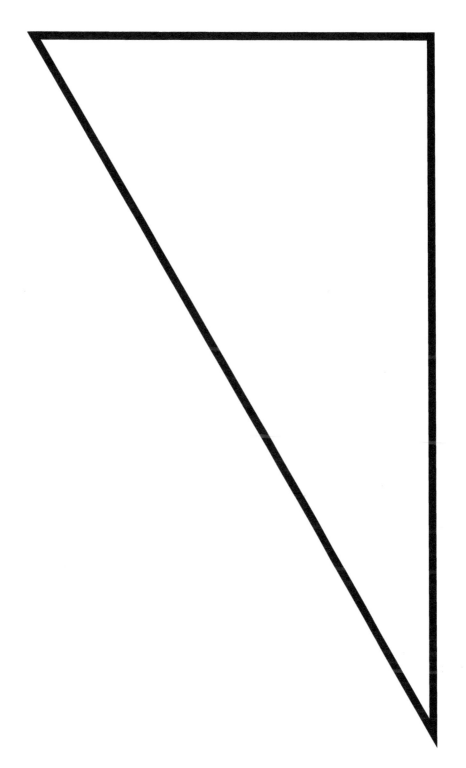

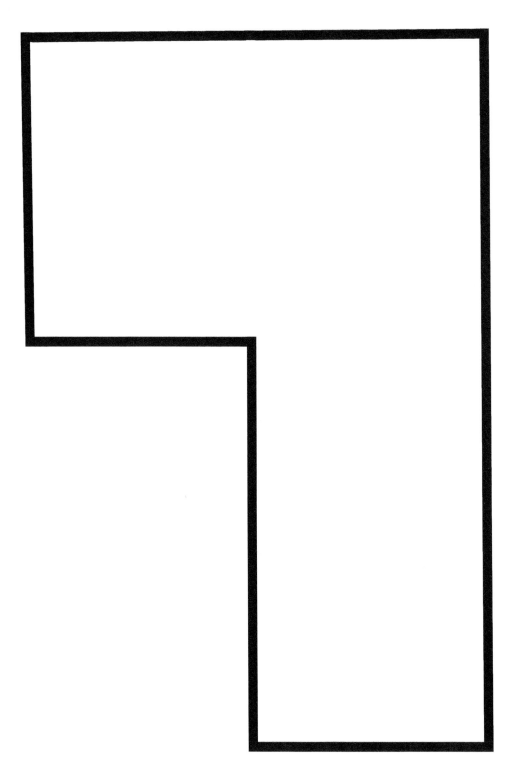

Make a Shape

Snapshot

Students work together to construct shapes that have particular components, beginning with shapes that have three straight sides.

Connection to CCSS
K.G.5, K.G.4, K.G.2

Agenda

Activity	Time	Description/Prompt	Materials
Launch	5–10 min	Tell students, "I made a shape with three straight sides." Ask, What might my shape look like? Tell students they are going to work with a partner and some materials to build what they think your shape could have looked like.	Materials for constructing shapes, such as paper, rulers, pipe cleaners, or toothpicks
Play	15–20 min	Partners work together to use materials to build figures with three straight sides. Encourage students to construct multiple solutions.	Materials for constructing shapes, such as paper, rulers, pipe cleaners, or toothpicks
Discuss	10–15 min	Partners choose one of their figures to share. Discuss how the partners know that the shape has three straight sides, and ask whether the class agrees or disagrees. Display those figures that the class agrees have three straight sides. Discuss how you could name this group of shapes.	Display space

Activity	Time	Description/Prompt	Materials
Extend	20–40 min, ongoing	Repeat this activity either as a whole-class routine or as a station or center, changing the components of the shape students make, either by increasing the number of side or by describing the number of corners instead. Discuss the group of shapes students create.	Materials for constructing shapes, such as paper, rulers, pipe cleaners, or toothpicks

To the Teacher

This activity is the flip side of the Visualize activity, in which students developed descriptive language for shapes and the aim was to grow increasingly attentive to the components of shapes. Here we frame students' work through those components and challenge students to construct multiple shapes with a given set of components, beginning again with triangles, or shapes with three straight sides. Constructing shapes that have particular parts is more challenging than analyzing a single existing shape, so you may want to delve into this activity only after students have had several experiences with the Visualize activity.

One of the aims of this activity is to provide an opportunity for students to see the diversity of shapes that meet any set of parameters. All too often, students are only exposed to particular versions of triangles, rectangles, or hexagons. If students only see equilateral triangles with a base parallel to the bottom of the page or floor, they come to think of this as the only true triangle, and later describe a rotated triangle as "upside down" when there is no up or down side to a triangle. Be sure students see examples of triangles where all three sides are different lengths, where no one side is parallel to the bottom of the page or bulletin board, and where there are no right angles. Although students don't yet have the vocabulary or conceptual understanding to describe this diversity, seeing it will keep their minds open about what makes a triangle, or any other shape.

Activity

Launch

Launch the activity by telling students, "I drew a shape with three straight sides." Ask, What could it look like? Give students a chance to turn and talk to a partner. Tell students that they are going to make a shape that could have been your shape, and show students the materials they have for constructing these shapes with a partner.

Play

Provide students access to materials for drawing or building shapes. Partners work together to make one or more shapes that have three sides. If students build their shapes, provide them with some way of mounting their figures to protect them and share them with others. This could mean taping them to pieces of construction paper or pinning each to a bulletin board.

As partners work, ask them questions about how they know the shape they have made or are making has three straight sides like the one you made. Ask, Is there any other way my shape could have looked? Encourage students to develop multiple ways of representing a three-sided figure.

Discuss

Invite partners to choose one of their shapes to share with the class. Ask the following questions:

- How did you know you had made a shape with three sides?
- Do we all agree? Why or why not?

Create a space to display the collection, adding shapes that the class agrees have three straight sides to the display as you go. Ask the class, What name can we give these shapes? Discuss whether students think they can all be called triangles.

Extend

This activity can be repeated, changing the components required to four straight sides, five straight sides, or three corners. You can do this activity as a whole class as a routine, or turn it into a station or center, collecting students' constructed shapes over several days and then talking about them.

Look-Fors

- **Are students attending to all of the parts of the task: three, straight, and sides?** Although the notion of constructing a shape with three straight sides may strike adults and older children as a single constraint because we are thinking of these shapes simply as triangles, for young children there are actually two different ideas here. First, the shape has to have three sides, and second, those sides have to be straight. As you talk with partners at work and later as you facilitate the discussion of whether the shapes have three straight sides, ask questions to focus attention on both of these ideas. You might ask, How did you know your shape had three straight sides? If students simply point and count, you might say, "I see from your counting there are three sides. How did you know they were straight?" Whether a side is straight should be based on the creator's intent, rather than on unrealistic expectations of precision.

- **Are students thinking of multiple ways they might solve this task?** One of the goals of this activity is to support students in seeing multiple versions of shapes that have the same features. You may see students using materials to construct or draw equilateral or right triangles first. Press students to think of new ways that they might make a figure with three straight sides by asking, What other shapes can you make with three straight sides? Could there be another way? You might even invite students to walk around the classroom with their partner for a moment, looking at others at work, to get ideas if they are particularly stuck.

Reflect

When you are building a shape that has to look a certain way, how do you begin?

Building Blocks

Snapshot

Students use a small set of pattern blocks to construct as many different shapes as they can, exploring the different ways that larger shapes can be composed of simple ones.

Connection to CCSS
K.G.6, K.G.4, K.G.1

Agenda

Activity	Time	Description/Prompt	Materials
Launch	15 min	Introduce pattern blocks and provide an opportunity for students to explore them. Create a chart of students' observations about the different pieces; the chart should show all six shapes.	• Pattern blocks, in containers, for students to explore, per partnership • Chart and markers
Explore	20+ min	Partners choose two or three pattern blocks from the set and use them to construct as many new shapes as they can. Partners trace each shape they create.	• Access to pattern blocks to choose two or three per partnership • Materials for recording
Discuss	15 min	Partners share the shapes they made from the two or three pattern blocks they selected. Discuss what makes a shape and come to a class definition for this word.	

BIG IDEA 3: TALKING ABOUT AND MAKING SHAPES

Activity	Time	Description/Prompt	Materials
Extend	30+ min	Show students the Triangle Turtle image and ask what they notice. Ask students how they could use the pattern blocks to construct a figure, like the turtle, that others would recognize. Provide access to pattern blocks, and photograph students' creations. Share these with the class and discuss what students notice, how the figures were constructed, and the ways students approached building their figures from pattern blocks.	• Triangle Turtle sheet, to display • Pattern blocks, for each student

To the Teacher

In this investigation, we use pattern blocks to build larger figures, exploring what different figures can be made from a small set of pieces. We invite students to choose just two or three blocks to use to construct larger shapes, because restricting which pieces students use enables them to see what variety of figures can be constructed by changing the orientation or position of the pattern blocks in relation to one another. If your students have not yet worked with pattern blocks, they will need time to explore them without restrictions on which they use and how. Although we offer some opportunity for students to make observations about the pattern blocks during the launch of this activity, we know this is not sufficient for a full exploration of the pieces. We encourage you to make time for students to play with this tool, to investigate what pattern blocks can do and how they are related.

In the extension, we offer a complex image of a turtle composed of triangles. Many similar images of real-world figures decomposed into geometric shapes can be found online if this image piques students' interest. We offer this image as an inspiration, not as a goal. You'll want to be clear with your students that this, and any other images you might use, are meant to get students' ideas flowing. Students may produce simple or elaborate figures; in either case, they are thinking about the ways that everyday objects or living things can be composed of geometric components.

Activity

Launch

Launch the activity by introducing students to pattern blocks, if they are not yet familiar with them. Provide partners with access to a sample of the pieces, in bowls or containers, and invite them to make observations about what they see.

Encourage students to use the language they developed in the Visualize activity to describe and compare the shapes. Be sure that students see that there are six different shapes in the set. Create a chart about pattern blocks that collects students' observations of them and shows the six shapes.

Tell students that they are going to explore how to use these pattern blocks to make new shapes.

Explore

Partners choose two or three pattern blocks from the set to use as their building blocks. Shapes can be different or the same. Partners explore the following questions:

- What new shapes can you make? Trace all the shapes you can make.
- How many different shapes can be made with your shape pieces?

As you observe students, engage them in conversation about their shapes by asking, How could you describe the shapes you made from these pieces?

If students appear to exhaust all ideas, you might press them by asking, Are there any other ways you could use these building blocks to make new shapes? If they believe they cannot, ask, How do you know that you cannot make any more shapes? When students are truly ready to move on, you can invite students to choose two or three new shapes and start again.

Discuss

Invite partners to share the two or three building blocks they selected and some of the examples of the different shapes they were able to make with them. Students undoubtedly will join the shapes in different ways, including along sides and at vertices.

As a class you can discuss the key question, What makes a shape? This is how mathematicians create definitions: they come to agreement about what the criteria are. Support the class in coming to a definition of what is and is not a "shape" in this activity. For example, students might say that the building blocks have to touch in some way to be a shape, and they may or may not have rules for how the blocks can touch (at side or corners). It is fine if students' definition does not match the definition that mathematicians use; rather, we want students to engage in the process of coming to agreement about the rule.

Extend

Show students the Triangle Turtle image, and ask, What do you notice? Students may notice the whole as well as the different shapes that compose the whole. Ask students, How could you use your pattern blocks to create a figure that we might recognize? Provide students with pattern blocks to build their familiar figures. We encourage you to take photos of these to share with the class later. Discuss the following questions:

- What do you notice about the figure?
- How have you used the pattern blocks to construct the figure?
- How did you think about the figure you wanted to make so that you could decide how to build it?
- Where did you start? What did you build next?

Look-Fors

- **Are students recording the shapes they create?** Recording the larger shapes students make from the pattern block pieces can be challenging fine motor work for kindergarteners. But recording the shapes students make enables them to look back at the collection of figures they constructed to determine whether they have truly made new shapes and to examine during the discussion the question of what makes a shape. If students are not recording, tell them that drawing what they made is a way of saving their thinking and that their ideas are important. Because students are working with a partner, they can each take on a role of holding the figure on paper and tracing that figure to make the process somewhat less frustrating.

- **Are students rotating, flipping, and joining the pattern blocks to create new combinations?** Working with only two or three pattern blocks limits the number of ways that these shapes can be combined into new figures; however, there are still a large number of possibilities. You may notice some students sliding the shapes into new combinations but keeping some aspect constant, such as keeping the square in the center or always orienting the triangle with an edge toward the bottom. If students appear to be running out of ideas quickly, press them to consider new ways by challenging what they are keeping constant. You might say, "What would happen if the square wasn't in the middle?" or "What shapes could you make if you turned the triangle?"

- **How are students describing the shapes they make?** When you talk with students about the shapes they are creating, ask students to describe the figures. Listen for descriptions that are holistic (such as "It's a house") and those that focus on the components ("It has five sides"). You are very likely to hear holistic descriptions in this activity, and although they should not be discouraged, ask questions to support students in extending their descriptions to the parts of the shape. This can sometimes be easier for students to do when looking at their tracing of the figure than the blocks themselves, because the tracing enables students to focus on the outline. This is an appropriate time to encourage students to make comparisons between figures. You might do this by simply modeling observations that compare shapes after students have described two they have made, such as "This shape had five sides, and so did this one. That's interesting."

Reflect

Which shapes do you think are the most useful for building larger shapes? Why?

Triangle Turtle

BIG IDEA 4

Seeing Numbers inside of Numbers

An important part of the brain is called the approximate number system, often abbreviated to the ANS. This is a part of the brain that focuses on one important function: converting a group of dots or objects into a number. Interestingly, this ability has been linked to higher mathematics achievement. This is just one of the reasons I am a big proponent of dot-card number talks, an activity I learned from mathematics educator Cathy Humphreys. In a dot-card number talk, you share a collection of dots with students for a short period of time. The reason it is a short time is that you want students not to count the dots but to use their ANS and estimate the number of dots by grouping them. Whenever I share dots with people, even a small number of people, I find that they see them in many different ways. This allows me to make an important point—that we all see mathematics differently, and even seven (or whatever number) of dots can be seen in a multitude of ways. I recently conducted a dot-card number talk with a group of middle-school girls, and they saw the seven dots I showed them in all of these different ways, shown in the figure, on the bottom row, fourth image from the right:

Source: From *Limitless Mind*, by J. Boaler, 2019, pp. 115–116. New York, NY: HarperCollins.

In a recent summer camp conducted with middle-school girls, they loved dot-card number talks so much they asked for them every day. It was important that they also took the approach of seeing a kind of pattern in many different ways and started to apply that approach to other patterns they saw, which I loved. An example of me teaching middle-school girls with a dot-card number talk is available at https://www.youcubed.org/resources/jo-teaching-visual-dot-card-number-talk/.

In our Visualize activity, we share a lesson plan for a dot-card number talk. Be ready—these activities can be mind-blowing for students and impact them in many positive ways. If this is your first time trying a dot-card number talk, you may find you want to do many more of them and incorporate this as a regular routine in your classroom.

In our Play activity, we continue with the big idea of seeing the ways numbers are made, this time giving students snap cubes of different lengths that can be broken in two to make two different numbers. The snap cubes give students something important—the experience of physically holding numbers in their hands, stimulating important and different pathways.

In our Investigate activity, we engage students in a game that asks them to decide which of two groups of dots is bigger. They are then asked whether they can think of ways to prove that the group they think is bigger is actually bigger. This engages students in another important mathematical act: proving.

Jo Boaler

Dot Talks

Snapshot

Students use dot talks as opportunities to decompose larger sets of dots into smaller ones, which they can subitize—that is, recognize the quantity at a glance.

Connection to CCSS
K.CC.5, K.OA.3, K.CC.4c

Agenda

Activity	Time	Description/Prompt	Materials
Launch and Explore	5 min	Introduce the structure of dot talks, and ask students to try to figure out how many dots they see, but to really focus on *how* they see the dots. Show a dot-talk image briefly.	Dot Talk sheet, to display
Discuss	10–15 min	Invite students to share how they saw the dots and how many they saw. For each student who shares, record their thinking on a copy of the Dot Talk sheet, using circles to show the clusters of dots that students saw. Come to agreement about how many dots are shown, and draw attention to the multiple ways students subitized to see those dots.	Dot Talk sheet, multiple copies to record student thinking
Extend	15 min	This routine can become a facilitated small-group activity, in which everyone gets to contribute their thinking. Consider showing the dots with magnets so that students can show how they moved the dots in their minds.	Dot Talk sheets, or magnets on a whiteboard

To the Teacher

Dot talks have become a widespread routine in early childhood classrooms and beyond, as visual versions of the number talks first described by Ruth Parker and Cathy Humphreys (2015, 2018). Sherry Parrish's (2010) book on number talks provides a host of dot talks that encourage students to think visually about number and learn to subitize. People subitize when they recognize the quantity of a group of objects without counting. For kindergarteners, the aim is for them to recognize groups of two and three objects by sight, regardless of how the objects are arranged, and to later learn to recognize larger numbers in particular arrangements, such as those shown on a die.

Subitizing with larger groups of objects, such as the ones shown in the dot talks in this activity, involves decomposing that group into clusters that students can recognize. For instance, with the dot talk that launches this activity, students can begin to see seven dots by noticing two groups of two dots and one group of three dots, or two groups of three dots and one extra dot. Seeing seven dots in multiple ways builds understanding of the larger number, how it is composed of smaller numbers, and that there are many equivalent ways of decomposing any number. Through these dots talks, students are simultaneously working on counting, number, equivalence, composing, and decomposing.

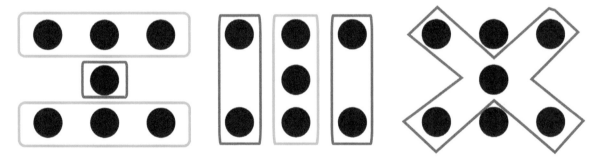

Three different ways students see 7

During the activity, you will want to ask students how many dots they see and ultimately come to agreement that no matter how they see them, there are a fixed number of dots. But, more important, you will want to emphasize the question, How do you see the dots? Even when students are not sure how many dots there are altogether, they can share with you ways of seeing the dots, clusters they notice, or ways the dots form shapes that help with counting, such as triangles or squares.

We encourage you to incorporate dot talks as an ongoing routine in your classroom, one that you can do multiple times each week. You will obviously need many more dot-talk images than we have provided here, which you can find in Parrish's book or make yourself. You'll want to include images that are organized and images where the dots are scattered. Recognizing the number of dots when scattered is far more challenging, so you will want to use fewer dots for those kinds of talks.

Activity

Launch and Explore

Launch the activity by telling students that you are going show them images of dots and ask them to figure out how many dots there are. Tell them that they may be able to figure out how many dot there are in all, or maybe they will just notice some of the parts. Tell students that after they have a chance to look at the dots, you will ask them how many they see, but mostly, you want to know *how* they see the dots.

Show students the first Dot Talk sheet briefly. Show it for long enough that students can pay attention to its structure, but not so long that students can count each dot individually. The idea is to encourage subitizing.

Discuss

After you put down the dot image, ask the following questions:

- What did you see?
- How many do you see?
- How did you see it?
- Which did you see first, the whole group or the parts?

For each student who offers one way of seeing the dots, post a copy of the Dot Talk sheet. Mark up the dots and label them to show the ways that each student sees the groups inside the larger number. Circle groups of dots that students saw as clusters and knew were two or three. Ask students, How did you put these groups together to find out how many dots there were altogether? Some students might have seen clusters but not have put the groups together. As a class, discuss ways to use the groups to figure out how many dots there are in the image. Be sure to highlight for students the key idea: we can see numbers inside of a larger number. One way to make this collection is to restate the different ways of talking about the dots in any image. For instance, you might say, pointing to the images you marked with students, "We agree this has seven dots. Another way to see it is that it has two dots and two dots and three dots. Or you can see it as three dots and three dots and one dot."

Repeat this process with other Dot Talk sheets from the collection provided, on this day or as an ongoing routine as part of math time.

Extend

You can do dot talks like these in small groups to vary the number of dots and whether they are structured or scattered. In small groups, there may be fewer strategies, but every student can contribute. Consider also trying these dot talks with magnets on a whiteboard so that kids can move them physically to show how they move them in their minds, if at all.

Look-Fors

- **Are students using reference objects such as dice or triangles to support subitizing?** As students learn to subitize, they draw on cultural and mathematical resources that organize objects. The most commonly used object in the US is the die, which organizes one to six dots in a regular structure that students may see in their lives in and out of school. When playing games with dice or dominoes, students may get repeated practice learning to subitize the dots, which can ultimately help them subitize in other situations, as in these dot talks. Similarly, students may draw on the implied shapes made by dots as the vertices, such as three dots forming a triangle or four dots forming a square, to recognize three or four dots. Be sure to draw students' attention to examples of using these kinds of resources to see the number of dots. Some may not realize that these are resources that they, too, can use until they hear about them from a peer.

- **Do students notice dots that are missing?** One strategy for figuring out how many dots there are involves seeing the dots as an arrangement with some dots missing. For instance, in the dot talk that launches this activity, one way to see the seven dots is to visualize the shape they make as a three-by-three square of nine dots, with one missing on either side. Most students will attend to the dots they see, rather than imagining additional dots and then compensating. So if this strategy emerges in your class, slow the discussion down and have the student share this thinking by pointing to the imagined dots, which you can draw in so that others can visualize what the student saw. Discuss why this strategy works, with questions such as, Why does it work to add dots in your mind? When might this help us?

- **Do you notice students referring to moving the dots in their minds?** One other strategy related to imagining extra dots is to move the arrangement of dots in your mind. For instance, in the dot talk that launches this activity, students could mentally bring the top left and top right dots down a row, so that the bottom two rows resemble the way six is presented on a die, with one extra on top.

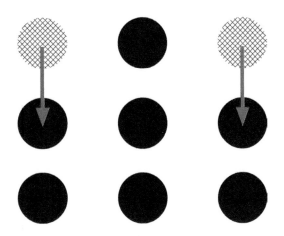

Seeing dots move to create a known pattern

Students often don't perceive that they have the power or authority to change the image mentally into one they can more easily count. But adjusting problems to include more friendly numbers or conditions is a universal problem-solving strategy that students can and will use for the rest of their lives. Just as with imagining dots, if you hear a student say that they moved a dot to a place that was more useful to them, slow the discussion down and draw attention to this as a strategy. Invite the class to imagine moving the dot(s) and what the new arrangement would look like. Ask the student who used this strategy to talk about why they moved the particular dot(s) they did and how they decided where to move them.

Reflect

When you see a group of objects (such as dots), what does your mind notice? How does that help you figure out how many there are?

References

Parker, R., & Humphreys, C. (2015). *Making number talks matter*. Portland, ME: Stenhouse.

Parker, R., & Humphreys, C. (2018). *Digging deeper: Making number talks matter even more*. Portland, ME: Stenhouse.

Parrish, S. (2010). *Number talks*. Sausalito, CA: Math Solutions.

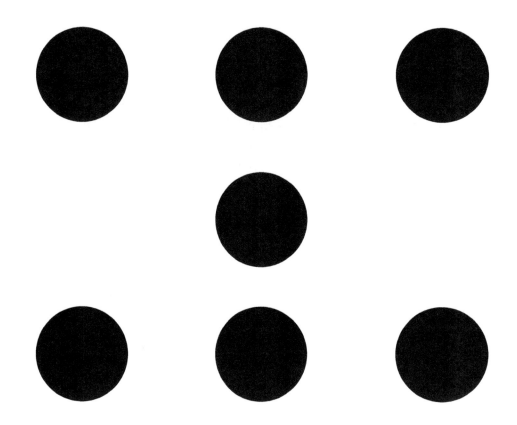

 **Dot Talk**

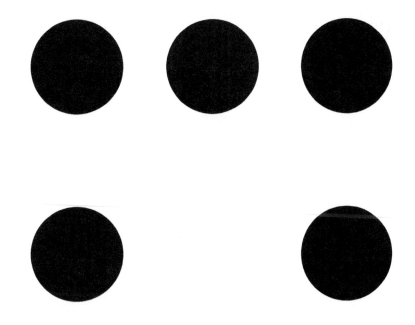

Dot Talk

Dot Talk

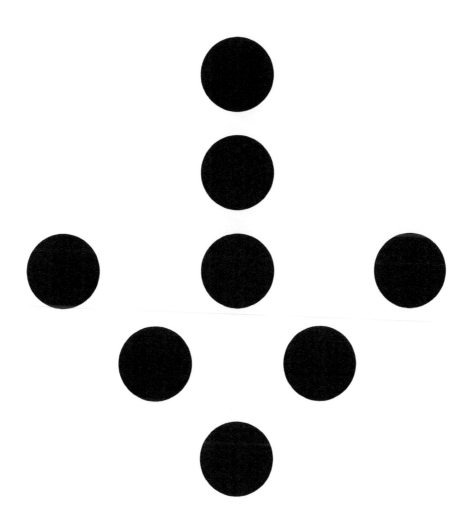

 **Dot Talk**

Dot Talk

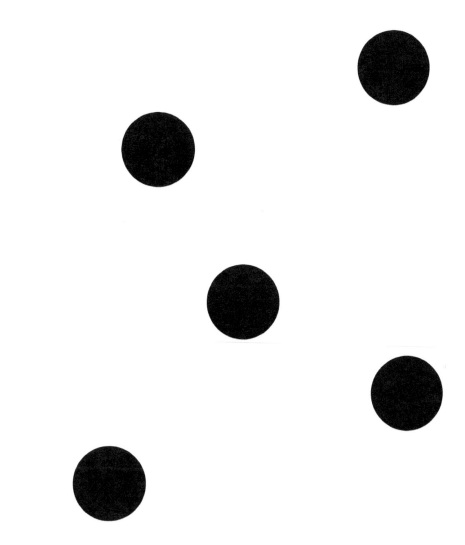

 **Dot Talk**

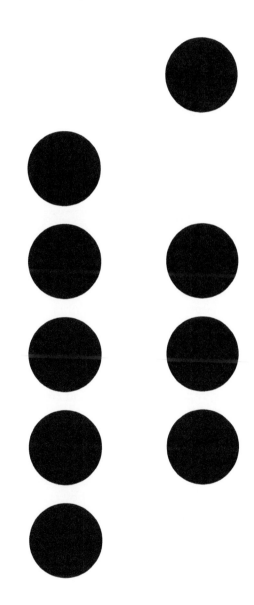

Snap It!

Snapshot

Students build understanding of how numbers can be decomposed and recomposed by playing a game of Snap It.

Connection to CCSS
K.OA.3, K.CC.5, K.CC.3

Agenda

Activity	Time	Description/Prompt	Materials
Launch	10–15 min	Play Snap It as a class. Show students a stick of snap cubes 4–10 cubes long, then break it. Discuss how many cubes are in each piece and altogether. Reconnect the pieces and snap the stick again in a new place, and discuss the same questions. Change the number of cubes in the stick so that it has 7–10 cubes, repeat the process, and create a chart of the results.	• 10 snap cubes • Chart and markers
Play	15 min	Partners play Snap It using the same number of cubes as in the stick at the end of the launch, trying to figure out how many different ways they can snap the stick into two parts. For each way they find, they record the number of cubes in each piece and the total to bring back to the group.	• Snap cube sticks, per partnership, the same length as the last stick explored in the launch • Index cards or sticky notes, per partnership
Discuss	10–15 min	Discuss the different ways students found to snap their stick of cubes into two parts. Chart students' ways and discuss whether they have found all the possible ways.	Chart and markers

Activity	Time	Description/Prompt	Materials
Extend	15–20 min	Turn Snap It into a partner game, in which partners take turns building a stick, snapping it, counting the cubes in each part, and counting the cubes in the whole.	10 snap cubes, per partnership

To the Teacher

In this activity, we use the game Snap It to focus on decomposing—and then recomposing—numbers up to 10. Building on the work students have done with dot talks in the Visualize activity, in this game students construct sticks of snap cubes that they break into two parts. Students grapple with how many cubes are in each part and how they come together to make a whole stick of cubes. By arranging these objects in a line, rather than in clusters as in dot talks, students are encouraged to think of numbers linearly, planting the seed for number lines later on.

Inherent to this work are part–whole relationships, and our aim is for students to see that the whole can be conserved even when it is decomposed in different ways. Students can examine the different ways to decompose a single number repeatedly, building a foundation for algebraic thinking. Students can discuss what makes for different ways to snap the stick, touching on commutativity. For instance, is 6 and 1 the same or different solution than 1 and 6? In some situations, the difference would not matter, as when rolling two dice. But in other situations, the order would very much matter, as when we ask, How could two friends share seven markers? Snap It does not have a context, so whether these are two solutions or one is a matter for students to discuss.

You can use Snap It as another whole-class routine, just as with dot talks, where you create, show, and snap a stick for students to count and discuss. This could be done in just a few minutes, and you could record solutions for students to see, accumulating them across days and weeks. However, we suggest that by allowing students to play this game with partners, you push students' thinking about the many ways to snap a single stick of cubes. We've included recording in the Play part of the activity as a way for students to see whether they have found new or repeated solutions, and as a way for you to observe the connections students are making between quantity, oral counting, and written numerals.

Activity

Launch

Launch the activity by telling students that they are going to be playing a game with cubes called Snap It. Show students a stick of snap cubes that is 4–10 cubes long. Be sure students have a chance to see the full stick, then break the stick into two sections while students observe. Ask students, How many cubes are in each piece? How many cubes were there in the full stick? Give students a chance to turn and talk to a partner about what they see. Invite students to share their thinking about how many cubes are in each piece and how many cubes there were altogether. Students can come up to point at or touch the cubes to count and prove how many there are.

After the class comes to agreement, put the two pieces back together, then snap the stick again in a new way. Ask students again, How many cubes are in each piece? How many cubes were there in the full stick? Discuss these questions until the class can agree.

For the next round, take some cubes away or add some until the stick has 7–10 cubes, and repeat this routine, being sure that students know you have changed the number of cubes in the stick. After students come to agreement about how many cubes are in each piece and altogether, make a shared record of what you learned about this stick. On a chart, draw the stick and show with a line how it was snapped; label the parts and the whole.

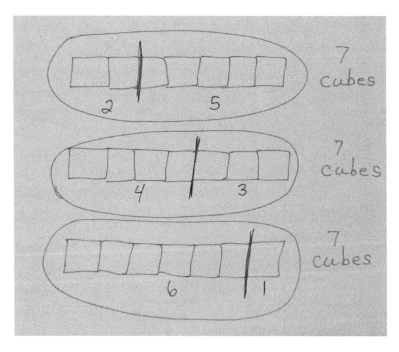

Teacher recording of different ways students
snapped their stick

Ask students what other ways they think they can break this stick into two pieces. Tell students that this is what they are going to explore in their game today.

Play

Provide partners with a stick of cubes the same length as the last one you explored in the launch, along with index cards or sticky notes. Partners explore the question, How many different ways can we snap this same stick into two pieces? For each way they find to snap the stick, they come to agreement about how many cubes are in each piece and how many cubes there are altogether. Partners record each way on an index card or sticky note so that they can see what new ways they have found.

Discuss

Gather students together, with their index cards or sticky notes, to discuss the following questions:

- What different ways did you find you could snap this stick?
- Can we find all the ways? How do we know when we've found them all?

For each solution students share, add it to your chart. You can give the chart a title, such as Ways to Snap a Stick of 8. Ask students, Did you find this way to snap this stick? Give students a chance to look through their solutions. You can invite students either to set that solution aside now that it has been recorded, or to add it to the chart next to your drawing of it. You may also want to discuss the question, How did you record your thinking? This creates the opportunity to examine ways that students have drawn and labeled their work and ways to show the total.

Extend

Make this into a partner game, with the following routine:

- Partner A builds a stick with no more than 10 cubes.
- Partner B snaps the stick.
- Partner A figures out and explains, How many cubes are in each part?
- Partner B figures out and explains, How many cubes are there altogether?
- Partners swap roles.

Students can play this game in partners at a center, or the whole class can play it simultaneously.

Look-Fors

- **Are students recognizing that the total number of cubes does not change?** As students snap the same stick repeatedly, we ask them to find how many cubes there were total. Students may continue to recount these cubes with each new way to snap the cubes, either because they are unsure of the total or as a way to check. However, some students may notice at some point that the total number of cubes is always the same. Ask students questions about how they knew how many cubes there were in the stick and listen for students conserving the total. This is something to return to during the discussion, that no matter how you snap the stick, the total number of cubes doesn't change. Many students will likely still want to recount to check that this is true; let them count to confirm this pattern as many times as they need to.

- **How are students describing the total and the parts?** Students need language for part and whole relationships. Listen in for the ways that students are describing the parts and how those parts compose the whole. You might hear words such as *altogether*, *together*, *total*, or *whole*. If students are struggling to find ways to describe how the two parts make something larger, step in to give them some words we use to describe this relationship. We might say, for example, that "these two parts make the whole stick" or, more specifically, "This part has three cubes and this part has four cubes. Together they make a stick of seven cubes." Be sure to draw on students' informal language to support these descriptions and make sure they have opportunities during the discussion to hear the different ways that students describe the part–whole relationship.

- **How are students recording their solutions?** Pay attention to what students record for each of their solutions. You'll want to look for how they are labeling the parts and the whole with numbers and whether they are using drawings. If students draw their sticks, which we would encourage, ask students to count their pictures aloud, just as they would their cubes, to check that their pictures match the manipulatives. Students can revise their recordings if needed. This will also give you a chance to hear their counting and see how they have matched numerals to the oral counting sequence. Be sure to look for the ways that students are indicating the whole in their recordings. They may use a circle around the two parts to show the whole, or redraw the stick, or invent some symbols.

Reflect

How can you use the number of cubes in the parts to figure out how many there are in the whole stick?

Which Is More?

Snapshot

Students use visual and counting strategies to compare groups of dots in a game of Which Is More?

Connection to CCSS
K.CC.6, K.CC.5

Agenda

Activity	Time	Description/Prompt	Materials
Launch	10–15 min	Show students the Two Sets sheet on the document camera and ask, Which group has more dots? Give students a chance to think and then turn and talk. Students share their thinking. Then ask, How could we prove which group has more dots? Invite students to develop some counting strategies. Introduce the game, Which Is More?	Two Sets sheet, to display
Explore	15–20 min	Partners play Which Is More? using the card deck. Partners make predictions visually about which group has more dots and then develop strategies to prove which has more.	Which Is More? deck of cards, per partnership
Discuss	10 min	Discuss how students could tell visually which group had more dots and the strategies they developed for proving which group had more.	

Activity	Time	Description/Prompt	Materials
Extend	15+ min	Turn Which Is More? into a partner game in a station or center. Partners can add new cards to the deck using the Make Your Own Cards sheet.	• Which Is More? deck of cards, per partnership • Optional: Which Is More? Make Your Own Cards sheet or blank laminated cards and dry-erase markers

To the Teacher

In this activity, we build on the ways that students see numbers inside of numbers in dot talks to compare two sets of dots in a game called Which Is More? Students compare two groups of dots drawn from a deck of cards, developing strategies for determining which group has more dots both visually and by using counting strategies. Students are likely to run into challenges with a few areas. First, students will likely struggle with the difference between a group that has more dots and a group that takes up more space. When we use the word *bigger*, it is not clear whether we mean more (number) or larger (area). We encourage you to be precise with your language by asking which group has more dots and to expect that this conceptual struggle will still arise.

Second, students are likely to struggle when the two groups have similar numbers of dots, such as six and seven, or when those dots are scattered. Both of these challenges make determining the difference between groups more difficult to do visually, and it makes sense that students may simply not be able to determine which group has more. Expect that "I'm not sure" will be an answer you might hear, and it is better to approach this by asking, Why? than by pressing students to simply guess. It will be useful for students to name that the two groups look too much alike or that it's harder to tell when the dots are scattered. This idea connects back to one of the reasons we organize for counting, something that came up in the first big idea and that the kindergarteners are talking about all year long.

For the cards, you can simply copy them and cut them out to make a paper deck, or you can make laminated decks. Beyond the laminated versions being sturdier, students can draw on them with dry-erase markers to show how they grouped or counted the dots, providing useful evidence for the closing discussion. Before you invite students to try this, you may want to wait until they have had some experience with the game.

Activity

Launch

Launch the activity by showing students the Two Sets sheet on the document camera. Tell students that there are two groups of dots here, a group of red dots and a group of blue dots. Ask students, Which group has more dots? Give students a chance to think independently and then turn and talk to a partner. Invite someone to share their thinking and how they thought about which one was more. At this stage, it's fine if that thinking sounds like, "It looks bigger."

Ask the class, How could we prove which group has more dots? Invite students to come up and count to prove which group is larger. We encourage you to mark up the sheet to show the proof students generate, including how they counted. Be sure to highlight strategies that students have used in dot talks to notice clusters of dots within the larger group.

Introduce the game Which Is More? and how to play. Tell students that their goal is to develop strategies (or ways) for figuring out which group is more by looking and by counting.

Explore

Provide partners with a deck of the Which Is More? cards. Partners begin by mixing up the cards and placing the deck face down where they can each reach it. Partners each draw a card, placing the two cards side by side where they can both see them. Partners then try to figure out which card has more dots by looking. Each partner gets a turn to say which one they think is more and why. Then together the partners try to prove which one actually is more, using whatever strategies they develop.

Students repeat this process for each round, drawing two new cards to place on top of the previous cards, predicting which is more and then developing strategies for proving. When the deck runs out, students can mix the cards again and start over.

Discuss

After students have had a chance to play, gather to discuss the following questions:

- How did you know which one was more?
- What strategies did you come up with for deciding which one was more?
- How did you prove which one was more?

These questions ask students to think generally about how they could tell which group had more dots, either visually or by counting. But students may find it difficult to talk in the abstract like this. If so, you can ask students to choose a pair of cards to show what their strategies were in specific cases, such as when the numbers were very close or when they were very different. During the discussion, draw attention to strategies that compare, break the dots into smaller groups, and use language of comparison such as *more than*, *less than*, *bigger*, *smaller*, *fewer*, and *same*.

Extend

Make this game available for students in stations or centers. Students can make their own cards to add to the decks using the Which Is More? Make Your Own Cards sheet. You can provide these cards to students for them to draw on, or laminate blank cards for students to draw on with dry-erase markers, so that the same blank cards can be used repeatedly.

Look-Fors

- **Are kids struggling to come to agreement, even when they are counting?** You may notice that even when students have counted the dots, they may still not agree on how many dots there are or which group has more dots. Support students by giving them counters that they can place on top of the cards so that they can move the dots to count and compare. Students can then place the dots in a line for each card, matching the counters to see which line has more dots. Alternatively, students may agree on how many are in each group but not on which is more. Ask, How can we tell which one is more? Is there a tool that could help, like counters or fingers? The counting sequence can be supportive here. If students count aloud, they can hear which number they say first and which comes after. This is a concept itself, that as you say numbers aloud, they get larger, which students may be developing in this activity.

- **Are kids using "bigger" to mean more dots or more space?** When dots are scattered, rather than organized, the same number of dots may take up more space on the card. This group can appear "bigger" because it occupies a greater area. One aspect of conservation is that students understand that moving the dots does not change the number, no matter whether they move them closer together or farther apart. Students may need to test this idea themselves. Consider offering students counters to represent the card, count, move around, and recount. Be sure to use precise language with students, so that instead of asking, Which group is bigger? you ask, Which group has more dots?

- **What grouping strategies are students using?** Students may use some of the counting strategies they developed in dot talks to support figuring out which group has more dots. For instance, students might cluster dots into smaller groups of 1, 2, and 3 to count the total. Alternatively, students might use these clusters to compare the larger groups. For instance, students might observe that, in the Two Sets image, the group of five dots is made of a cluster of two and a cluster of three, but the group of seven has two clusters of two and a cluster of three. By comparing these smaller clusters, they may never consider how many dots are on the card. This is an inventive and very mathematical way of thinking about the task. Be sure to draw attention to these ways of using clusters of dots to count and compare.

- **How do students handle equal groups?** It may happen that students draw two cards with the same number of dots, though represented differently. Watch closely how students handle and name what they see, and be sure to raise this with the whole group during the discussion. This is a prime opportunity to build the language of *equal*. In this setting, the two groups are the *same*, but only in quantity or value, not in appearance. This is the essence of equivalence. It is why we can say that 2 + 3 is equal to 5; they do not appear the same, but they have the same value. If you hear students observe that two groups are the same, ask, How are they the same? You might observe that they don't look the same, to prompt students to think more precisely about what they mean. Use this as an opportunity to introduce the word *equal* as a word for "same number or quantity."

Reflect

When you see two groups, how can you tell which group has more?

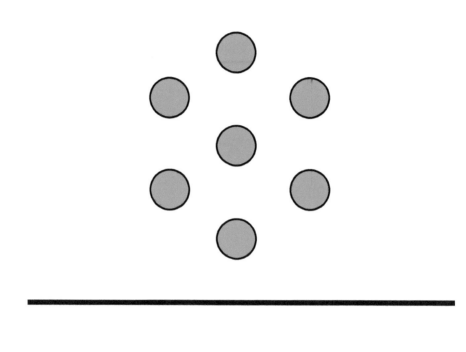

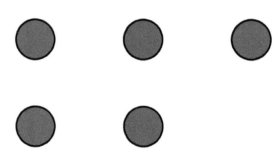

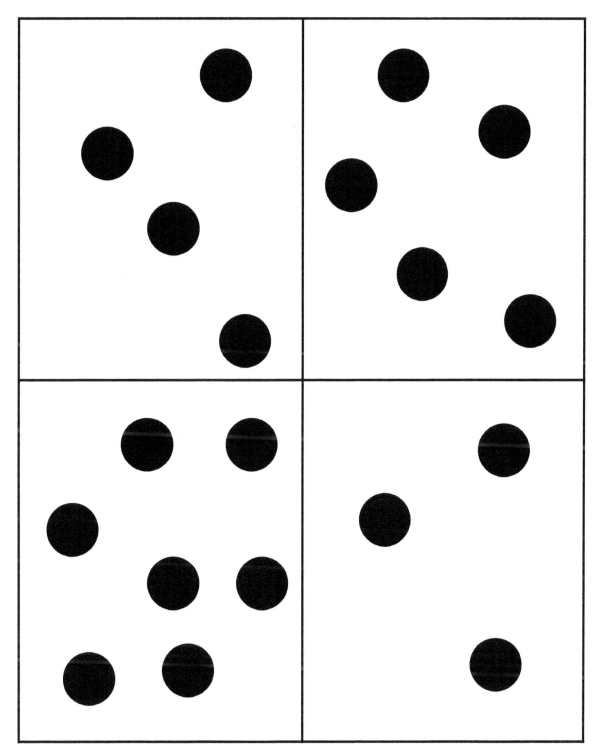

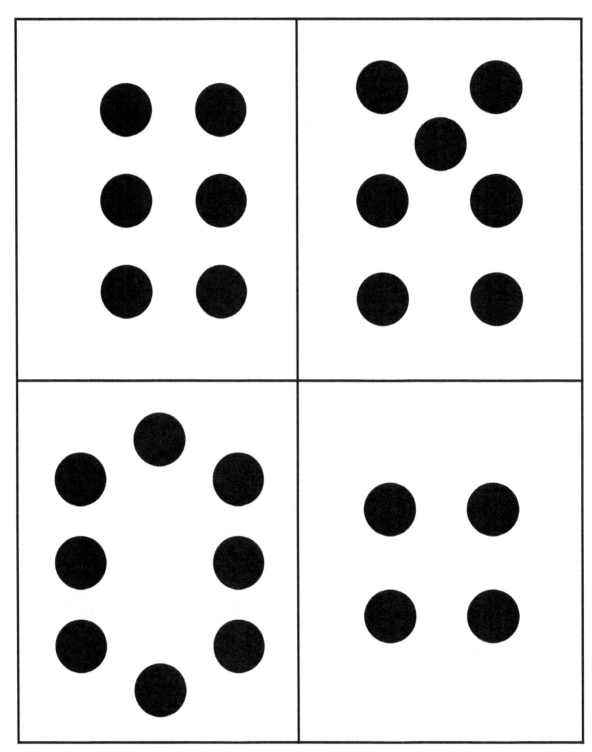

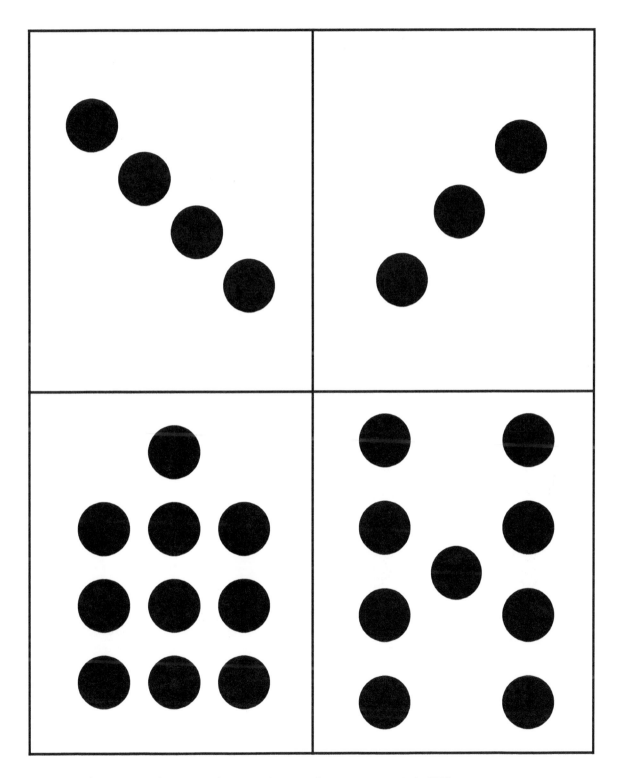

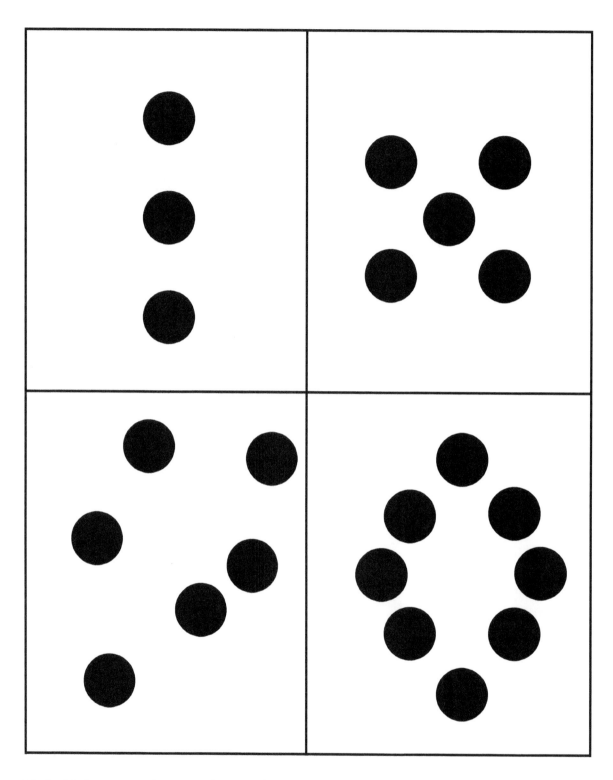

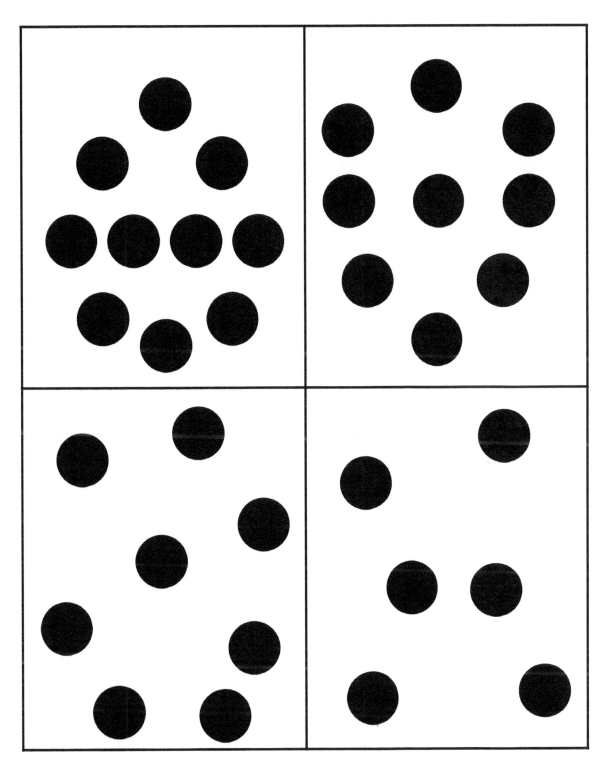

Putting Numbers Together

In our earlier activities, students met and interacted with numbers through work with dots and their fingers. These are important foundational activities. In this big idea, we extend students' understanding of number and the very important development of number sense through work with counting and adding. It is important that these activities are visual and help build the interactive brain pathways that come about when visuals are connected with numbers. We know from research that the most important number understanding that students need is number flexibility; when students are flexible with numbers, they can break them apart and be playful with them (Boaler, 2019). Instead of adding 7 and 4, a student may decide to add 5 and 2 and 4, breaking the 7 into a 5 and a 2. Some students go through school thinking that numbers are inflexible, that they are only there to be used with rules, and that if you are given a 7 you must use a 7. That kind of thinking limits students' mathematical growth, and it is very important that students learn that they can act on numbers and be flexible with them. As students enter the realm of addition, keep as a goal the creation of opportunity for students to be flexible with the numbers they are using.

In our Visualize activity, students will see a block pyramid and be asked to continue the growing pattern. Students notice and describe the growing pattern and work to understand the way it grows through adding on a different number each time. See whether students notice that the pattern keeps its shape as it grows, and ask them to think about the number they add on each time. This is a pattern that could generate amazing kindergarten thought.

In our Play activity, students get to work with dice. This is a lovely way for students to see numbers as dot patterns and to have fun while they are thinking about them. It is also an activity that brings students into the world of data science, as they generate their own data from dice. You can talk to the students about the importance of data in our world (for more information, see https://www.youcubed.org/resource/data-literacy/). Students roll dice and plot them on a number line—another important mathematics tool that we bring in to help students develop number sense.

Our Investigate activity is one that we have shared on our Youcubed website and that is loved by teachers and students. Students will be invited to make their own parade. The combination of all the parades can make a beautiful wall display with many different ways to see ten. This is a great beginning for the development of number flexibility.

Jo Boaler

Reference

Boaler, J. (2019). Developing mathematical mindsets: The need to interact with numbers flexibly and conceptually. *American Educator*, *42*(4), 28.

Growing Bigger and Bigger

Snapshot

Students grow a pyramid pattern made from squares, figuring out how many to add on and how many squares compose the pyramid, to connect the ideas counting and joining numbers.

Connection to CCSS
K.OA.1, K.OA.2, K.CC.5, K.CC.1, K.CC.2

Agenda

Activity	Time	Description/Prompt	Materials
Launch	10–15 min	Show students the pyramid shape made with squares and ask what they see. Discuss how students see the shape and the number of blocks used to make it. Discuss how you might grow the shape and how many squares you would need to add on.	Square tiles or blocks in multiple colors
Explore	15–30 min	Partners explore ways to build and grow the pyramid shape. As they grow the pattern, students record the figure, how many squares they have added on, and how many squares make up the full pyramid.	• Square tiles or blocks, per partnership • Pyramid sheet and colors, per partnership
Discuss	10–15 min	Students share their ways of recording the growing pyramid and what they noticed as they added on to the figure. Discuss the strategies students developed for finding the total number of squares in the shape.	
Extend	20+ min	Partners design their own growing shapes with squares. They work to grow the pattern, layer by layer, recording the shape, how many they add on, and how many squares make up the figure.	Square tiles or blocks and colors, per partnership

To the Teacher

As you introduce ideas around joining and separating numbers, we highly recommend that you use the work of Cognitively Guided Instruction (CGI) as described in *Children's Mathematics* (Carpenter et al., 2015), which is based on decades of research into how students develop conceptual understanding of whole-number operations. We see this Visualize activity, and indeed all the activities in this big idea, as a companion to CGI, in which children explore a variety of joined and separate problem types drawing on contexts familiar to them in their worlds. As the teacher, you are best positioned to craft those problems, building on your knowledge of your students and community.

In this activity, we draw on a truly splendid example of spontaneous mathematics that Angela Andrews and Paul Trafton (2002) described in their book about kindergarten math, *Little Kids—Powerful Problem Solvers*. In that experience, students built towers out of plastic cups and tried to figure out how many it would take to reach the ceiling. We've adapted this idea here to build a pyramid pattern out of square tiles or cubes, growing the pattern ever larger. This infinitely extends the range of numbers that students are joining, far larger than what the standards call for in kindergarten, but we do not want to limit students' exploration. Some students may struggle as the numbers get larger, but counting is a key resource for joining; and this activity will press students to count ever-larger groups, connecting the concepts of joining and counting. Do not feel the need to move quickly into ideas of addition as an operation; it is enough to explore what it means to "add on some squares" and find out how many you have now.

Activity

Launch

Launch the activity by building a pyramid with blocks that has three levels, like the one shown here. You can do this in two dimensions with square tiles, or in three dimensions with cubes.

Ask students, What do you see? How many blocks are there? Discuss these questions as you would in a dot talk, attending to both what students notice about the structure of this pyramid and how many blocks they count. Be sure that students notice that the shape has a structure with three layers, though students may see the layers differently. Most students will notice the layers horizontally, but some may see the layers moving left to right or vice versa.

Then ask students, How can we add on to this shape and grow it? Tell students that you still want it to look like this shape, only bigger. Give students a chance

Three-level pyramid made of wooden blocks

to turn and talk to a partner about how and where they could add on new blocks. Invite students to come up and show how they would do it using extra blocks or tiles. Students might add on a row underneath or along the ridge on one side or the other. Be sure to ask students whether they have other ways to grow the pattern and discuss how they know that it still has the same shape.

Ask students, How many did we add on? How many blocks are in our pattern now? Give students a chance to turn and talk to each other, before telling them that this is their challenge today. They will be growing this shape or pattern, one layer at a time, trying to figure out how many blocks to add on and how many are in the pattern altogether.

Explore

Provide partners with blocks or square tiles, a Pyramid sheet, and colors. Be sure students have access to a sufficiently large space to build their pyramids. Partners use the tiles or blocks to build the pyramid pattern and then explore the following questions:

- How can we add on to this pattern and grow it?
- How many did we add on?
- How many blocks are in our pattern now?

Partners can build the pattern as large as they want, recording on the sheet to show how it grows and how many blocks there are. Students may count all, count on, or try to put numbers together, all of which are appropriate strategies. If students want to grow their pyramid larger than the paper, then tape on additional pieces of blank paper to support recording.

Discuss

Gather students and invite partners to share their pyramid records on the document camera or floor. Discuss the patterns they found, using the following questions:

- What happens when you add on to this pattern or shape?
- How many did you add on? How many were there in the pyramid then?
- How did you know how many to add on?
- What strategies did you use for finding how many blocks were in the whole pyramid?

Be sure to draw attention to the strategies students used for figuring out how many blocks were used in the whole pyramid each time. For instance, students may have counted the entire shape each time; others may have used what they learned from the previous layer to count on.

Extend

Invite students to create their own patterns with squares, such as staircases or herringbone, and then grow that pattern. Provide access to square tiles or cubes, paper, and colors. Students first build the beginning of a pattern or shape with blocks and then try to draw it. Then, each time they grow the shape, partners think about how many they will need to add on and figure out how many squares they have altogether in the pattern then. Encourage students to develop ways to record their patterns, counts, and thinking.

Look-Fors

- **Are students seeing the structure of the pyramid?** In the launch and as you observe students working, you'll want to pay attention to how students see the structure of the pyramid. Students will need to recognize that each row of the pyramid increases by one, following the counting numbers. No matter how they see the pyramid growing, whether by adding rows on the bottom or layers to the left or right, the first layer has one block, the second layer has two blocks, the third layer has three blocks, and so on. The blocks are arranged in a staggered pattern, which can be challenging for students to notice and reproduce. They may at first only notice that each layer or row is bigger than the last, and may build it with each layer growing by two instead of one, so that the blocks line up. Draw students' attention back to the Pyramid sheet or the shape you have created and ask them to compare what they have made to the original. Ask, How are these alike? Are they different in any way?

- **How are students finding the number of squares in the pyramid? Are students counting all or counting on?** Listen to partners as they talk about how many squares there are in each row and, particularly, in the whole pattern. Many students will see finding the total number of squares as a counting task, starting back at the top of the pyramid and counting all the squares anew each time. Similarly, some students may add a row of squares to the pyramid until it looks right, and then count how many they have added on. Some students may use patterns to predict how many squares will be needed in a row, and others may count the total by counting on from some point in the pyramid. For instance, they might use their count from the previous round as a starting point, or use the knowledge that there were six squares in the original three-layer pyramid, counting on from there. Ask students about what they are doing, and then invite them to share these ideas during the discussion. This is the beginning of using the structures of number to move beyond counting.

- **How do students handle the pattern when it grows large?** If students continue to grow the pyramid to six layers, they will have more than 20 squares in the figure, with each additional layer making the total swell further, faster. For some students, this will represent an interesting challenge to their counting, and you may find that students have questions, such as, "What comes after 39?" Support students in using the oral counting sequence, and if you have a number line or other resources in the room, you can point students toward those as a reference. For some students, these larger numbers may be frustrating. Encourage students to continue to build the pyramid and to figure out how many squares are in each row they add on. You can also ask students to label their count of the squares until they aren't sure what to write. This provides useful formative assessment data on students' ability to count, which will continue to grow as they have opportunities, like this one, to stretch their counting horizons.

Reflect

What strategies did you come up with for figuring out how many squares were in your shape?

References

Andrews, A. G., & Trafton, P. R. (2002). *Little kids—powerful problem solvers: Math stories from a kindergarten classroom.* Portsmouth, NH: Heinemann.

Carpenter, T., Fennema, E., Franke, M. L., Levi, L., & Empson, S. (2015). *Children's mathematics: Cognitively guided instruction.* Portsmouth, NH: Heinemann.

 **Pyramid**

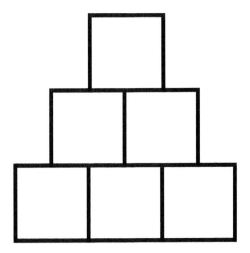

Roll the Dice

Snapshot

Building on subitizing, students develop strategies for joining numbers by playing Roll the Dice and using a line plot to record the total number rolled.

Connection to CCSS
K.OA.1, K.CC.5, K.OA.5, K.CC.3, K.MD.3

Agenda

Activity	Time	Description/Prompt	Materials
Launch	10–15 min	Introduce students to dice. Practice safe ways to roll them. Collect student observations about the dice, including the number of dots on each face. Play Roll the Dice as a class and show students how to use the line plot sheet to record the number of dots they rolled.	• Die, one per student • Roll the Dice Line Plot sheet, to display • Colors • Optional: chart and markers
Play	20+ min	Partners play Roll the Dice, working together to figure out how many dots they have rolled on the two dice. Partners use the line plot sheet to record the number of dots they rolled, playing until they have rolled all the values 2–12. Students make observations about the line plot.	• Dice, two per partnership • Roll the Dice Line Plot sheet and colors, per partnership
Discuss	10 min	Discuss the strategies students used for figuring out how many dots they rolled on the pair of dice. Look at the line plots together and make observations.	

Activity	Time	Description/Prompt	Materials
Extend	15–45 min	Turn Roll the Dice into a game partners can play at a station or center. You can extend the game to be played with three dice and invite students to develop their own line plot sheet to record the results. Discuss the differences that emerge when playing three dice and what new strategies students need for finding the total number of dots rolled.	• Two or three dice, per partnership • Roll the Dice Line Plot or grid paper (see appendix), per partnership

To the Teacher

In this activity, we are building on the subitizing work students have been developing through dot talks to introduce students to dice. Dice are a cultural object with consistent arrangements of dots. In the US, dots are arranged on dice like those shown in the picture, but in other cultures that have dice, the dots may be arranged differently. If you have students whose families have different cultural traditions with dice, we encourage you to invite them in and have students notice the different ways numbers can be represented, just as you would with a dot talk.

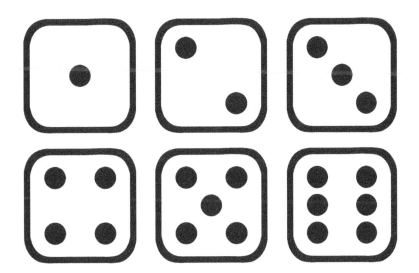

Source: Shutterstock.com/Krisztian.

Dice encourage subitizing as students learn to recognize the familiar arrangement of each number and the patterns between the numbers. Students will notice, for instance, that the 3 is an extension of 2, and that 5 and 6 are built on the arrangement of 4. By rolling two dice and figuring out how many dots they have altogether, students begin to join numbers, but have individual objects—the dots—to count, rather than being confronted with only numerals. Students can develop visual and counting strategies for joining the groups of dots, which we encourage you to discuss with students after they have had a chance to play the game.

Activity

Launch

Launch the activity by introducing students to dice, if they have not yet used them in your class. You may want to ask students whether they have ever used dice before and what they already know about dice. Show students how to roll dice safely and give students an opportunity to practice. Invite students to look at the dice and make observations. You may want to make a chart to record students' observations about the dice, including the number of dots on each face.

Play Roll the Dice as a class, so that students understand the process of rolling, discussing, and recording. Show students how to use the line plot to record the number of dots they roll. Students can mark the squares above each number with Xs or by coloring in the box. Tell students that after they have played the game many times, they will be able to use this recording to see what numbers they have rolled.

Play

Provide partners with a pair of dice and a Roll the Dice Line Plot sheet. Partners play the game by rolling two dice. Partners discuss the following questions:

- How many dots are on the dice altogether?
- How do we know?

Partners mark the Roll the Dice Line Plot sheet with the total number of dots rolled. Partners continue rolling until they have gotten every number 2–12 on the line plot. Then partners discuss what they notice about the numbers they have rolled.

Discuss

Gather students to discuss the following questions:

- How did you know how many dots you rolled? (Invite students to share strategies.)
- When you were trying to get all the numbers on your line plot, what happened?

In this discussion, be sure to highlight the ways that students were counting, subitizing, or simply recognizing the number of dots on the face of each die. When putting the two dice together, students may have used a variety of strategies to join the numbers, including counting all, counting on, or using known facts, such as knowing what one more than any number is or that 2 and 2 make 4.

Look at the line plots together. You may want to post all of them in a display space, or choose a few to represent the class's work. Invite students to look at what different partners rolled when playing the game. Ask students, What do you notice? This conversation serves as an introduction to looking at data. It is not the goal here for students to come to conclusions about why some values are more frequently represented than others. Rather, encourage students simply to make observations and pose questions.

Extend

Make Roll the Dice a game that students can play with a partner at a station or center. Students can play repeatedly to build fluency with subitizing and joining, and to explore the patterns the class observed in the data. The game can be extended to include three dice, but note that the Line Plot sheet will no longer be sufficient. Students can create their own recording sheet using grid paper (see appendix), which is an exploration unto itself. Partners explore the following questions:

- How many dots can you roll with three dice?
- What happens when you play this game over and over? What do you notice on the line plot?
- What is different about playing with three dice? What is the same?
- What new strategies do you need in order to figure out how many dots there are?

Look-Fors

- **Are students subitizing?** Listen in for instances of subitizing. You may hear students recognizing the whole die, saying, "That's 2," or students may decompose the die into parts. For instance, students might see the 6 as 3 and 3. One of the goals of working with dice is for the arrangements of the dots to become increasingly familiar and, ultimately, useful tools for decomposing groups of objects. If you notice that students are not subitizing at all, it is worth making note. Students will nearly all recognize 1 and 2, but you may see students counting even these. If you do, you can ask questions to investigate, such as, "Is there a way to know how many there are without counting?" or "I noticed that you counted these dots, 1, 2. Why did you decide to do that?" Some students may count simply as a check; others may be doing so as the beginning of a count-all strategy for the pair of dice.

- **What joining strategies are students trying with different numbers?** Working with dice offers students the opportunity to join numbers without them being represented by numerals. Instead, students have two groups of dots that they can count. You may see a variety of strategies, including counting all; even when students recognize the individual dice as, for example, 2 and 3, they may still return to count all: 1, 2, 3, 4, 5. The more opportunities students have to count all, the more restless with this method they will get, moving toward the more efficient count-on strategy. Look for examples of students counting on to share with the class, such as students seeing 2 and 3 on the dice and counting 2, 3, 4, 5. Students might also transfer the dots to their fingers, counting all or counting on using the fingers in place of the dots. Although this may seem a simple act, it is a kind of abstraction that will be useful in the future and worth noticing for the class. You may also see some joining strategies, either based on the dice or using known facts. For instance, students might see that a 2 and a 3 look just like the 5 when joined together. Or students may know that 2 and 2 make 4. These strategies represent a trajectory of ways that students might engage with joining the dots, and students need lots of opportunities to move toward fluency with joining any numbers.

- **Are students understanding what the line plot represents?** The line plot is likely a new representation for students, and it may take some work to interpret. Students will need to understand that each box above a number represents one time that the dice totaled that number of dots. Conversely, if no boxes are marked, this means that that value has not yet been rolled. When you sit down to talk with partners, watch as they move to mark their value. Does the numeral match the number name they gave the total? Are they marking the next available box vertically, moving from the number up the page? Ask students to tell you about what they have rolled so far, using the line plot as evidence. Are students able to describe what the different markings mean? If students are struggling to use this tool, take them back to the example you did together in the launch and have students retell what happened. Support students in recording their roll and making sense of why they are marking the space they do.

Reflect

What strategies were most useful for figuring out how many dots you had rolled altogether? Why?

Roll the Dice Line Plot

2	3	4	5	6	7	8	9	10	11	12

Foot Parade

Snapshot

Students create multiple ways to compose and decompose 10 by constructing parades where the animals have a total of exactly 10 feet.

Connection to CCSS
K.OA.2, K.OA.4, K.OA.3, K.OA.1

Agenda

Activity	Time	Description/Prompt	Materials
Launch	10–15 min	Discuss parades and show students the animals that can be part of their parades. Come to agreement about how many feet each animal has. Tell students that they will be making animal parades with a partner where the animals have a total of 10 feet.	Parade Animals sheet, to display
Explore	20+ min	Partners create parades with 10 feet using the Foot Parade Cards. Students explore the different parades they can make, how they know they have 10 feet, and what the longest or shortest possible parades are.	• Foot Parade Cards • Paper • Tape or glue stick, per partnership
Discuss	10–15 min	Invite students to share some of the parades they made and how they knew they had 10 feet. Discuss what the solutions have in common and what makes them different, including differences in length.	
Extend	20–45 min	Partners construct new foot parades, with 10, 12, 15, or 20 feet as the goal. Discuss the ways students used 10 as a benchmark to help them create parades with more feet, and the different strategies they developed.	• Foot Parade Cards • Paper • Tape or glue stick, per partnership

To the Teacher

In this activity, we invite students to explore the many ways they can compose or decompose 10. Students design animal parades, a series of animals, who together have a total of 10 feet. We've provided animal choices with 1 (snail), 2 (ostrich), 4 (moose), 5 (starfish), 6 (lady bug), and 8 (octopus) feet. Using these animals, students create a sequence for their parade with exactly 10 feet in all. Some parades will be short, with only two animals; others can be as long as 10 snails. These do not represent all the ways to decompose 10 into groups of numbers, and this may come up in your conversations with students. For instance, students might notice that if they use a snail, there is not a single other animal they can pair with it to reach 10 feet. That is, there is no animal with nine feet. This can become fruitful ground for discussion.

Although we've selected these animals with mathematical intention to offer many interesting combinations, they may not be the animals that most excite your students. If you are studying particular creatures or habitats in other parts of your day or you have local species you'd like to represent, you can revise the animals included in the task. We encourage you to select animals with 1, 2, 4, 5, 6, and, if possible, 8 feet.

Finally, although we have designed this investigation to explore ways to decompose 10 because of the role 10 plays in our place value system, you can extend this task by changing the target number of feet in the parade. In the extension, we suggest 12, 15, or 20 feet, but students could also chose their own number to investigate and represent in multiple ways.

Activity

Launch

Launch the activity by telling students that they are going to make a parade of animals. If students don't know what a parade is, spend some time talking about how people march in a parade to celebrate a holiday or event. You may have one in your own community to use as an example.

Tell students that in their parade, instead of people walking, there will be animals. Show students the animals they have to choose from to be in their parade by displaying the Parade Animals sheet on the document camera. Tell students that there are lots of differences between these animals, and one thing that makes them different is the number of feet they have. Ask, How many feet do each of these animals have? Give students a chance to turn and talk to a partner, and then discuss each animal as a class. Come to agreement about how many feet each animal has. Label these on the Parade Animal sheet.

Tell students that their parades must have a total of 10 feet. They can choose any animals, but they can only have 10 feet in each parade they make—no more, no less.

Explore

Provide partners with Foot Parade cards, paper, and tape or a glue stick. Using the animals provided, partners explore the following questions:

- What animals can make a parade of 10 feet?
- What's the longest parade you can make with 10 feet?
- What's the shortest parade you can make with 10 feet?

Partners make parades and attach their solutions to paper. Invite students to label the numbers of feet on each animal. Partners can work together to construct multiple parades, each on its own piece of paper and with a total of 10 feet.

Discuss

Gather students and their parades to discuss the following questions:

- How did you make your parade so that it had exactly 10 feet?
- What different parades can be made with 10 feet? (Invite students to share some of their parades and how they knew that they had 10 feet.)
- What do our different solutions have in common?
- Are there any parades that are very different? How?
- What are the shortest parades we made? Why are they so short?
- What are the longest parades we made? Why are they so long?

You may want to designate a display space for the parades where you can group them to show similarities and differences, or arrange them by size. During this discussion, highlight the different ways that students thought about composing or decomposing 10. Students may have noticed particular animal combinations that worked well together, or patterns, such as "All the parades with the octopus are short."

Extend

Make this activity a center or station and change the number of feet possible in the parade. Consider trying 12, 15, or 20 feet. Note that odd numbers will press students to use the snail or starfish, while even numbers don't require these animals. You can create space for students to display parades of different lengths by having a board for 12-foot parades and one for 20-foot parades. Be sure to discuss with students how they had to think differently to construct parades with more feet and notice how they might use 10 as a benchmark for creating parades with more feet. For instance, students might take solutions for the 10-foot parade and simply add on two snails or an ostrich to make 12 feet, or double a 10-foot parade to make 20 feet.

Look-Fors

- **Are students accurately attending to the number of feet?** To solve this parade problem, students will need to understand how many feet each animal has and focus attention on those feet, rather than other features, such as how many animals there are. Watch students as they work to construct their parades and listen for counting feet or considering the number of feet. You might see students touching each foot, referring to the labels you made on the Parade Animals sheet, or touching a single animal while saying the number of feet. Intervene early on if you notice that students are focused on the number of animals instead of feet or if you see that they misinterpret how many feet a given animal has.

- **Are children using the same animal more than once?** Students sometimes assume that they can only use each animal once, but many more solutions (and some mathematically interesting ones at that) are possible if they understand that they can use the same type of animal multiple times. For instance, it is useful to see that two starfish, with 5 feet each, make a 10-foot parade. Observe the parades that students are constructing, and if you notice that there no repeated animals, ask them questions such as, "Do you think you could make a whole parade out of one kind of animal?" Be sure that they understand that this is allowed and even encouraged as a way of thinking about the numbers.

- **What combinations are students creating that might be useful ways of thinking about 10?** Learning to decompose 10 is a central concept in kindergarten and beyond, ultimately supporting students in thinking about ways to join and separate numbers using place value. Each time students have a parade that is nearly finished and they ask themselves, "How many more feet do I need to make 10?" they are engaging in critical mathematical work. Furthermore, some of the combinations that students discover are mathematically quite useful in the long run. For instance, students need to know combinations of 10 that they might see here, such as 5 and 5, 4 and 6, and 2 and 8. Repeated combinations are the beginning of multiplicative thinking, such as discovering that five animals with 2 feet make 10. Be sure that students have the opportunity to share these kinds of combinations and the ways they thought of for closing the gap between the number of feet they had in a parade and the 10 they needed.

Reflect

How did you choose the animals to be in your foot parade?

Foot Parade Cards

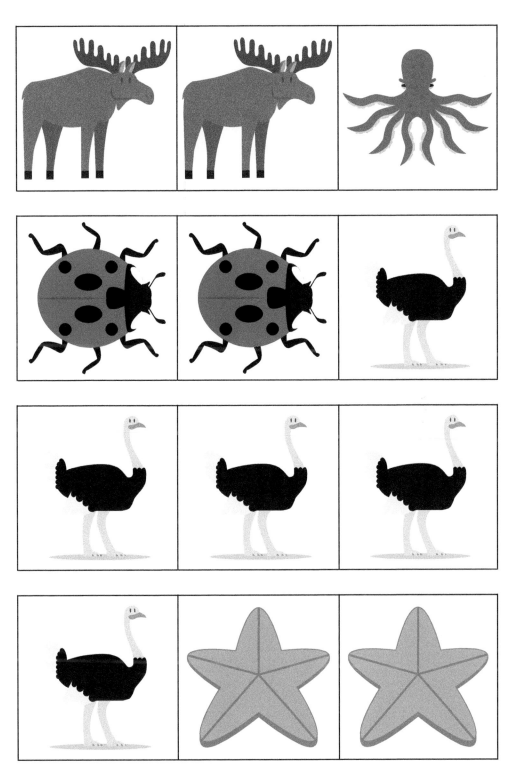

Foot Parade Cards

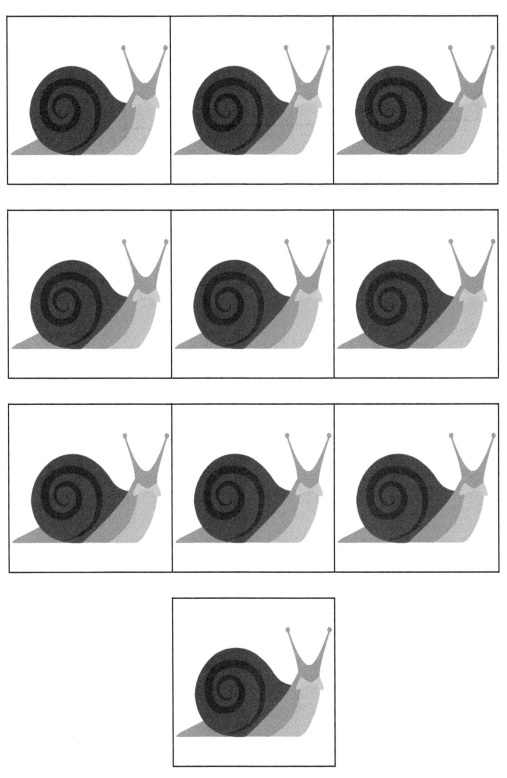

Describing and Sorting Objects

The mathematical demands of our modern world have changed dramatically over the last few decades, but the mathematics we teach in schools has not changed much at all. One of the areas of mathematics that is really important for our students' futures is data science. An incredible 90% of the world's data was produced in the last two years, giving us some sense of the changing world students are entering (for more information, see https://www.youcubed.org/resource/data-literacy/). All major employers hire data scientists, and 7 of the 10 fastest-growing jobs have the word *data* in their description. The mathematical methods that help students make sense of data, and begin a journey in data science, are in the Common Core and other curriculum, but they are often ignored by textbooks and some schools. The data science journey begins in kindergarten, and young students should be encouraged to develop data sense alongside number sense. This big idea is centered on an important aspect of data sense—the act of classifying objects, choosing attributes, and sorting.

In our activities in this big idea, we do something many books do not: we ask students to choose the attributes by which they sort the objects we give them, and to justify their choices. Justification is another critical mathematical act, one that kindergarten students often do not get to experience. After students have chosen how to sort, they record their sorting, which is another important part of data sense.

In our Visualize activity, students are shown an image and asked to share their thinking, communicating how they think objects are sorted. After they have experienced this as a class, they are given their own collection of objects to sort. It is a key aspect of this activity that students are given choices to make and are asked to communicate and justify their choices. They are also asked to quantify their sorting and to do some data recording.

Our Play activity is modeled after our popular Youcubed lesson—sorting emojis. Students are given a set of emojis that are on individual cards to sort. They can sort by different attributes that might include emotion. Students can make their cards into a display to explain how they sorted. It is good to focus on the descriptions students use to explain.

In our Investigate activity, students get to sort buttons. Students first see an image of some button sorting that another child organized. They are then invited to sort buttons in their own way, again communicating the attributes that they choose. A muffin tin can be helpful, as it enables students to view the sorted buttons.

Jo Boaler

Sorting Supplies

Snapshot

Students explore attributes by developing ways of sorting school supplies into groups.

Connection to CCSS
K.MD.3, K.MD.1, K.MD.2, K.CC.6

Agenda

Activity	Time	Description/Prompt	Materials
Launch	5–10 min	Show student the Sorted Supplies image and discuss what it means to sort or organize objects. Students make observations about how these supplies are sorted, noticing that type, size, and color are involved.	Sorted Supplies sheet, to display
Explore	20–30 min	Partners develop strategies for sorting a small plastic bag of jumbled supplies. Students draw and count the objects in each group they made and compare the number of objects in each group.	• Small plastic bag of mixed supplies (such as paper clips, coins, erasers, rubber bands, or binder clips), per partnership, with some extra • Make available: containers for sorting, such as cups or bowls • Tools for recording, such as paper and pencils

Activity	Time	Description/Prompt	Materials
Discuss	10+ min	Discuss the different ways students did or could have sorted their objects, highlighting the different attributes students used. Students share how they counted, represented, and compared the groups they made.	
Extend	Ongoing	Create a station or center with a large collection of mixed objects for students to sort collaboratively over the course of a day or week. Discuss as a class, at any point, how students have decided to sort and why, and what other ways to sort they may have tried.	• Large collection of mixed items for sorting • Containers for sorting, such as cups or bowls

To the Teacher

For this activity, you will need to prepare small plastic bags of supplies for students to sort so that you have at least as many bags as partnerships in your class. The bags should contain at least three categories of items (such as paper clips, erasers, binder clips, rubber bands, magnets, colored paper clips, or coins) and no more than 10 items in any category. In addition to the variation of objects, you'll want to include some objects that have differences in their attributes, which create new possibilities for sorting. For instance, you might have small and large paper clips, or rubber bands of different colors. Students can sort the objects by type but also by size, color, purpose, or even material. Be sure that the collections are not all the same so that when students try new collections, new ways of sorting open up.

Encourage students to think about creative ways to sort, and look for opportunities to press students to sort groups a second time. That is, if students make a large group of paper clips, you might ask whether there is a way of sorting the paper clips into groups. This kind of hierarchical sorting, where the objects in a group share multiple attributes (for instance, they are both paper clips and large), is particularly challenging for students at this age. When students do this, however, they are recognizing that each object can simultaneously have multiple attributes that interact and intersect.

Activity

Launch

Launch the activity by showing the Sorted Supplies image on the document camera. Talk about what it means to sort or organize. You might say, "These supplies are sorted (or organized). What does that mean?" Give students a chance to turn and talk about what *sorted* means in this example, and then discuss this idea as a whole group. Come to agreement that sorting means making groups of things that are alike.

A sorted collection of supplies
Source: Shutterstock.com/Madlen.

Ask, How are these sorted? What do you notice about how these supplies are grouped or organized? Again, give students a chance to turn and talk to a partner, and elicit some ideas from the class. Students might notice that paper clips are together, for instance, but be sure they also notice that attributes, such as size and color, were used to make groups.

Explore

Provide partners with a small plastic bag of mixed school supplies and access to cups, bowls, or other tools for grouping objects as options for supporting their sort. Partners work together to sort out the jumble by answering the question, How could you organize these supplies? Partners will need to discuss how to sort the objects and come to agreement on what groups they will use.

Once partners have sorted the objects into groups, provide them with tools for recording their thinking, such as paper and pencils. Students explore the following questions:

- How many objects are in each group you made? How can you record the objects in each group? (Encourage students to develop pictures with labels to represent each group.)
- Which group has the most objects? Which group has the fewest objects? How do you know?

Although we encourage you to invite students to draw their groups of objects, for some students this might be a fine motor burden, and some objects are very hard to draw. Use your judgment to decide what is appropriate for your students at this point in the year. You might choose instead to take a picture of the sorted objects so that the image can be shared with the class.

After students sort and count, they can explore sorting again by doing the following:

- Mixing their objects up and finding a new way to sort the same objects
- Getting a new collection to sort, if you have enough
- Putting their objects back in the bag, mixing them up, and trading with another group

Discuss

Gather students together to discuss the following questions:

- How did you decide how to sort your objects? (Invite students to show the ways they sorted their objects and talk about the decisions they made.)
- What are the groups you made? (Be sure to highlight the different ways that students might have created groups. They may have made groups of all objects that are the same [e.g., paper clips] or used an attribute [e.g., made of metal].)
- Could you have sorted your objects in more than one way? What ways could you have sorted?

- How did you count your objects once you sorted them? Which objects had the most? The least? (Invite students to share the representations they made and how they used them to figure out how many were in each group or to compare the groups.)

Extend

Make a station or center with a large jumbled collection of objects for students to visit and work on together to create one or more sorting systems over the course of a day or week. The collection should include at least six categories of items and up to 20 items in each category. Provide bowls, cups, or other containers for sorting into groups. Consider this a collaborative project that you can then talk about as a class once the sort is complete or at any point along the way. Discuss the following questions:

- How did we decide to sort?
- Why did we choose that way?
- What groups did we make?
- What other ways of sorting did we try?

Use this discussion as an opportunity to highlight any new attributes that students decide to use to sort or examples of double sorting, where groups are defined by multiple attributes.

Look-Fors

- **Are students using attributes, rather than types of objects, to sort?** When students are new to sorting, it makes sense that they would begin sorting by the most obvious features of objects, their type. You will likely see students putting paper clips with paper clips and erasers with erasers. Just this initial sorting is cognitive work because students must decompose a jumbled group and see that there are groups hidden inside it. However, as students gain experience, sorting by type will become a much simpler cognitive task. You may see students attending to other attributes, such as size, color, material, texture, or even function, such as objects that squeeze. Be sure to highlight these when talking with students as they work and during the discussion. If you notice students who quickly sort by type, press them for other ways they might sort the objects so that they might consider attributes. You might say, "I see you've put all the paper clips together, all the erasers together, and all the magnets together. That is one way to sort these. Can you find another way?"

- **Are any students sorting by more than one attribute?** As we mentioned in the To the Teacher section, sorting by multiple attributes is a key conceptual leap that you should look for and encourage when opportunities arise. If, for instance, you have given students a group of magnets of different sizes, shapes, and colors, and they have grouped them all together, you might ask, "Is there any way you could sort the magnets into groups?" Then support students in describing any new groups they make, such as big magnets and little magnets, or round magnets and not-round magnets. If you find that students are already sorting by more than one attribute, be sure to discuss these groups with them, highlighting the multiple attributes the groups have in common, and inviting students to share this thinking during the discussion.

- **How are students comparing the quantities in their groups?** We have asked students to compare the quantities of objects in the groups they make. Students are also asked to draw their groups and label them. This provides several different points at which students might make comparisons and multiple tools they might use, including the objects themselves and their representations of them. Are students determining which group has more or fewer by counting the groups aloud? Alternatively, do they line up the objects side by side to compare the groups? Do they compare them visually? Do they use the numeral labels on their drawings to compare? These are all different ways to make comparisons, and each can lead to different kinds of mistakes. For instance, if students compare visually or by lining objects up, they may ignore differences in the size of the objects. Six binder clips may look much bigger than eight paper clips, for example. Comparing numerals is the most abstract of these comparison methods, and for this reason can lead to simple mistakes in forgetting which numerals represent which numbers. Talk to students about how they are making their comparisons between two groups and then multiple groups to figure out which has the most or fewest. Pay attention to the challenges they encounter that you might like to discuss as a class.

Reflect

How can you sort objects?

Mindset Mathematics, Grade K, copyright © 2020 by Jo Boaler, Jen Munson, Cathy Williams.
Reproduced by permission of John Wiley & Sons, Inc. *Source:* Shutterstock.com/Madlen.

Sorting Emojis

Snapshot

Students play with sorting faces showing different emotions, and the class works together to deduce how others have sorted these emojis.

Connection to CCSS
K.MD.3

Agenda

Activity	Time	Description/Prompt	Materials
Launch	5 min	Show students the Emoji Collection sheet and invite students to make observations about what makes the faces different from one another.	• Emoji Collection sheet, to display
Play	15–20 min	Provide partners with a set of the emojis cut into cards for them to sort in multiple ways. After students have explored different ways to sort the faces, ask them to glue the faces down into groups showing one way they can be sorted.	• Emoji Collection sheet, cut into individual face cards, per partnership • Construction paper and glue stick, per partnership
Discuss	10–15 min	Partners show their sorted groups, and the class discusses how they think the groups might be sorted. Ask the sharing partners to explain their thinking and then add labels to the groups to describe each.	

Activity	Time	Description/Prompt	Materials
Extend	15–20 min	Turn this activity into a station or center in which students can explore new ways of sorting the emojis. Students can modify existing emojis or create their own to make new possibilities for sorting.	• Emoji Collection sheets, cut into individual faces • Make Your Own Emoji sheets, cut into individual faces • Colors • Construction paper and glue sticks

To the Teacher

In this activity, we provide a new set of objects for students to sort, emojis. Your students may or may not have seen these symbols before, which are designed to convey particular emotions. Make time in the launch to ensure that all students perceive these faces as showing emotions, particularly if students are new to these symbols or struggle to read emotions on others' faces. These emojis offer very different ways of sorting as compared to the school supplies in the Visualize activity. Here students can attend to the emotions being shown and whether those emotions are enjoyable (positive) or not (negative). They can also focus on each image as a drawing with (or without) particular features. Students might notice, for instance, that mouths can be open, closed, or missing. Similarly, eyes can be open, closed, or winking. Faces may or may not include eyebrows or glasses. Each of these observations offers possibilities for sorting. In this activity, we want students to explore multiple ways to sort the same group, something they may not have had the chance to do with the school supplies.

The discussion is designed to get students to engage with one another's sorts and deduce the attribute that defines each group. This is a very difficult task that we think students will be more prepared to attempt after having sorted and re-sorted the same faces themselves. Be sure that when you invite students to show their sorts, they know that they are not supposed to explain them yet. Instead these become a puzzle for the class to solve. You may need to ask questions to scaffold the discussion, such as focusing attention on only one group of faces and asking, "What do these faces all have in common?"

Activity

Launch

Launch the activity by showing students the Emoji Collection sheet. Ask students, What do you notice about these faces? What makes them different from one another? Give students a chance to turn and talk to a partner, and then take some observations from the class. Students might notice differences in the emotions the faces represent, or in the parts of the faces, such as the eyes or mouths.

Play

Provide partners with the Emoji Collection sheet cut up into individual face cards. Ask, How could you sort these emojis into groups? As you walk around, ask students how they decided on a method to sort the emojis. Students can sort the emojis into two or more groups, depending on what attributes they attend to. Invite students to sort the faces, and then mix them up again and create a new sort to explore multiple ways the faces could be sorted.

After students have had a chance to sort a few times, provide partners with a piece of construction paper and a glue stick. Ask partners to choose one way to sort the emojis and glue them onto the paper in these groups.

Discuss

Invite partners to show their sorted emojis on the document camera without explaining their sort. Discuss the following as a class:

- How do we think these emojis are sorted?
- What groups do you see?

Come up with ideas as a class about how they might be sorted and then ask the partnership who created the sort to explain what they were thinking when they sorted them. Add a label to students' groups that describes how they were sorted, such as "Open eyes" or "Good feelings."

Extend

Create a station or center for students to continue to explore ways to sort emojis. You can continue to use the collection we have provided; substitute emoji stickers, which are widely available; or invite students to create new emojis using the Make Your Own Emoji sheet. Provide colors, construction paper, and glue sticks.

Challenge students to create more than two groups when sorting these emojis. Encourage them to add new features to their own or existing emojis to create new ways to sort. For instance, students might add a hat or nose to some emojis so that they can sort by these features. Students can glue their groups onto construction paper and then label each group with a descriptive name.

Look-Fors

- **Are students re-sorting the emojis using different attributes?** After students have sorted the faces once, they may be reluctant to mix them up or sort using a different attribute. You may notice that students simply repeat the same sort. Ask, What are some new ways you could sort these faces? You might have to be specific about what students have already done to encourage them to try something new, such as "I see you've focused this sort on the eyes. What else could you pay attention to, to sort these faces a different way?" If students do not want to lose their ways of sorting, you can photograph them so that students can know they have not disappeared.

- **Are students figuring out what groups of faces have in common?** The discussion may pose challenges for students; looking at groups of objects to determine what they have in common requires some ways of thinking that students may not have exercised yet. For instance, students need to ask themselves specific questions, such as "Are all the eyes open or closed?" or "What's going on with the mouths? Are they doing the same thing?" or "What are these feelings, and do they have anything in common?" This requires decomposing the faces into features to examine and doing so systematically enough that you might stumble on a shared attribute. Although we don't expect that individual students will be systematic, students as a class may be able to ask themselves enough questions about the images to find a shared attribute, unless it is particularly obscure. In facilitating this discussion, you may find it useful to ask students to share what they have wondered and discarded, not just what works. For instance, you can ask students, What parts have you paid attention to, even if you found that they didn't have anything in common in this group? By making the questions that students investigate more public, you will help students start to ask themselves similar questions that can support them in findings shared attributes.

Reflect

How was sorting faces different from sorting supplies?

Make Your Own Emojis

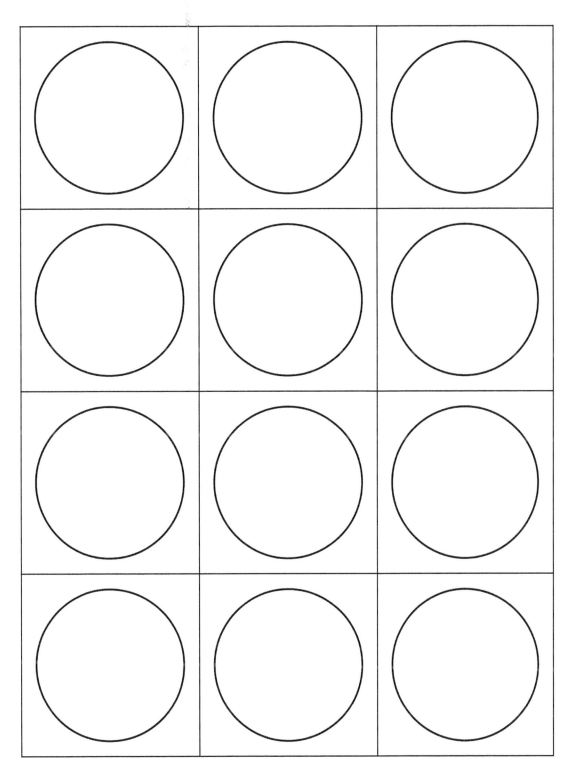

Sorting Buttons

Snapshot

Students investigate the many attributes of buttons and create groups to sort diverse button collections.

Connection to CCSS
K.MD.3, K.MD.1, K.MD.2, K.G.1, K.CC.6

Agenda

Activity	Time	Description/Prompt	Materials
Launch	5–10 min	Give each pair of students one button and ask them to make observations about it together. As a class, discuss some of the features that students noticed and make connections between the different buttons students examined. Highlight some of the attributes of buttons.	• Buttons, one per partnership • Optional: chart and markers
Explore	20–30 min	Partners examine a collection of buttons and discuss groups they could make. Together they sort the buttons into multiple groups based on their attributes.	• Collections of several dozen buttons, per partnership • Muffin tins, cups, bowls, or containers, for organizing sorted buttons
Discuss	10–15 min	Discuss the different ways students developed to sort the buttons, highlighting sorting rules that used multiple attributes. Make a chart of attributes for sorting buttons.	Chart and markers

Activity	Time	Description/Prompt	Materials
Extend	Ongoing (sorting station), or 15 min (small group)	Two possible extensions: make a sorting station with a large collection of buttons for the class to sort collectively over the day or week; alternatively, do a small-group activity in which students try to figure out how a collection of sorted buttons was grouped.	• Large collection of buttons • Muffin tin, cups, bowls, or containers, for organizing sorted buttons • Labeling tools, such as sticky notes or masking tape • Chart of button attributes from the discussion on display

To the Teacher

In this investigation, we explore another new item that can be sorted in a variety of ways, buttons. We love buttons for sorting because they have a large number of attributes for sorting, and large quantities can be purchased from craft stores or websites inexpensively. Once you have a collection of buttons, they can be used repeatedly for years. In a large, diverse collection of buttons, you will find buttons that vary by color, size, shape, number of holes, texture, material, and decoration. Students may also notice that some buttons have a raised ridge around the edge or words imprinted on the surface, while others do not. Some may be shiny or have a pearl finish, while others are matte. Some have a loop on the back where they are sewn on, while others have holes. Some may be transparent, with or without color. The number of attributes is simply huge, and each button can be sorted along multiple dimensions.

A collection of buttons has many different attributes for creative sorting.
Source: Shutterstock.com/Viktor Gladkov.

For each partnership, you will need to prepare a collection of buttons to sort. Each collection should have a large number of diverse buttons, at least several dozen, so that students have many ways to sort. It is important to note that students do not need to sort the entire collection for this activity, unlike with the school supplies and emojis in the earlier activities. They can simply use the buttons as a pool to draw from in creating groups with particular attributes. This is a time to encourage using multiple attributes. Take, for example, the button sort one kindergartner made here. Some of the categories focus on a single attribute, such as "Big buttons," while one intersects two attributes, "Buttons that are little and green." You'll notice that these are not comprehensive categories, which is to say that not every button in the collection could go into one of these categories. Students are likely to create groups by exploring the buttons available, noticing features, and then looking for others that share that feature. Encourage students to develop as many categories as they want as they explore.

These descriptions were provided by the student who sorted the collection:

1. Big buttons
2. Red buttons
3. Buttons that are little and green
4. Blue buttons
5. Transparent buttons
6. Buttons that are not flat

A sorted button collection

You'll notice in this image that a muffin tin was used to sort buttons. We think these are a handy way to organize multiple groups if you have some pans available. They encourage thinking about more groups, are about the right size, and are tough to knock over. If you don't have access to muffin tins, you can use cups, bowls, or other containers.

Activity

Launch

Launch the activity by giving each pair of students one button and asking them to look closely at it. Ask, What do you notice about your button? Give students a chance to talk with their partner about their button.

Invite students to share what they noticed about their buttons. As students make observations, such as "It has two holes," ask the class, "Who else has a button with two holes?" Support students in making connections between the attributes of their different buttons. Be sure students notice more than just the color or number of holes of the buttons. You may want to make a chart that shows different attributes of buttons by sketching some of the buttons students have and pointing to and labeling their features. You may need to provide students some language for attributes they notice.

Explore

Provide each partnership with a collection of buttons and a muffin tin or several cups for sorting.

Partners talk about ways they can sort the buttons in their collection. Encourage partners to take time to just look at the buttons before they begin. Then partners use the tools provided to organize the buttons into groups. Keep in mind that they may not sort all the buttons.

As you circulate to talk to students about their work, ask students to name the groups they have created. You might ask, How do you know what buttons go in this group? Can you find another button that could go in this group? Alternatively, you might ask students to find a button that doesn't go in any of their groups and talk about why. Use this time to circulate and observe as an opportunity to discuss with students attributes that they may not have considered.

Discuss

Gather students together and discuss the following questions:

- How did you sort your buttons? (Talk about the rules students used to sort them. Make, or add on to, a chart of different attributes for sorting buttons.)
- What other ways could we have sorted the buttons? (Highlight sorting rules that students used or could use that intersect multiple attributes, such as white buttons with two holes and white buttons with four holes.)

As students are explaining the ways they sorted their buttons, you may find it useful to have students bring their collections over to the carpet to show. This may be particularly useful when students have sorting rules that involve multiple attributes.

Extend

We offer two possibilities for extending this activity. In either, we suggest that you post the chart you made with the class during the discussion of button attributes for students to use for reference.

First, you can turn this activity into a station or center with a very large, diverse collection of buttons for students to sort. The collection should have hundreds of buttons to expand the ways that students might sort. Provide access to containers for the sorted groups. If you'd like students to build on one another's groups, encourage students to label their groups with a sticky note or masking tape and leave their groups behind when they leave the station, so that others can add on to the groups they have started. At the end of the day or week, you could discuss the different groups that emerged from this collective sorting process.

Second, you can build on the deductive work we began in the Play activity, by setting up a small-group activity with a presorted set of buttons and asking students to figure out how the buttons were sorted. Working in a small group, students can discuss what they notice about the buttons in each group and come up with a label they can apply to each group they figure out. You can facilitate by asking students what ideas they have about what each group has in common and exploring the buttons in that group to test their ideas.

Look-Fors

- **Are students using a variety of attributes to sort?** If students decide to use a single attribute to sort all the buttons, they have the opportunity to sort all the buttons following a single strategy. For instance, if students decide to sort their buttons by color, creating groups for red, orange, yellow, and so on, all buttons can be sorted using this scheme. However, once students have explored this way, encourage them to try new ways of sorting so that they attend to different kinds of attributes. You might do this by asking students to mix up their buttons and start again, or by asking them if they could separate one of their groups into some smaller groups, such as "red buttons with two holes" and "red buttons with four holes." Be sure to let the ways of sorting come from students. Students may find it easier to consider this process if you put all the buttons currently in one group back on the table so that the buttons can be physically sorted in different ways.

- **Are students able to describe the rules used for each group they create?** As you talk with students about their sorts, you'll want to ask them to describe each group they are creating. Listen carefully for how students describe these groups. You may hear hesitant or imprecise language that you can support with words that students may not have had the need for in the past. For instance, students might tell you that a group of buttons "has this bump" or "isn't flat" as ways of indicating the raised ridge or ring that runs around the circumference of the button. You may want to offer students the word *ridge* or *edge* to help them describe and define the group. In other cases, students may have descriptions, but they may be ambiguous in ways that are worthy of discussion. For instance, students may have groups of "big" or "little" buttons, but how big or little does a button need to be to belong in the category? Ask students about these fuzzy boundaries to invite them to think more about what these words mean to them in relationship to the buttons.

- **Are students using multiple attributes to construct groups?** As with the previous activities in this big idea, thinking about how attributes intersect is a goal of this investigation. Look for instances of students defining groups with multiple attributes to share with the class during the discussion. If you notice these, you may want to press students about what other groups they might need in relationship to the group they defined. For instance, in the sort shown in the To the Teacher section, the student created a group of "buttons that are little and green," which might point toward the need for a group of "buttons that are big and green" or "buttons that are little and black." By contrast, if students are using a simple rule for sorting that creates a small number of groups with a large number of buttons in each (e.g., "blue buttons" and "buttons that are not blue"), then use this opportunity to press students to find groups inside these larger groups, as discussed earlier.

Reflect

What other objects in the world could be sorted? How might you sort them?

Mindset Mathematics, Grade K

BIG IDEA 7

Seeing and Making Patterns Everywhere

Many people think that mathematics, the subject, is about rules and procedures. I think of mathematics as the study of patterns. The world is filled with beautiful patterns that we can appreciate on a daily basis, and I choose to find and appreciate patterns whenever I can. But I also see patterns in other mathematical ways—because every mathematical algorithm or method is really a pattern that always works. For example, if I ever need to multiply an even number by 5, I can divide the number by 2 and multiply it by 10. For example, 18×5 is the same as 9×10. This is a pattern that always works, in the same way that the formal algorithm for multiplication that involves "carrying" numbers is a different (less beautiful!) kind of pattern that always works. Mathematics is all about patterns, and kindergarten is a key time to help students see that an essential role for them is being a pattern seeker. These days I spend a lot of my time in hotels, traveling around the country—and the world—spreading our mathematics revolution (www.youcubed.org). This has allowed me to see that hotels love to decorate with mathematical patterns—the carpets and floors are almost always made up of patterns—and the wall art is often pattern based too. But patterns are not only in hotels; if you take a walk through nature or the streets of a town, you will see patterns in flowers, trees, paving stones, buildings, lights, and more. Keith Devlin (1994), a Stanford mathematician, has written a lovely book called *Mathematics, the Science of Patterns: The Search for Order in Life, Mind, and the Universe*, and in the book he talks about the pattern-based nature of our world. Mathematics is a lens that we can use to see the world; and when we do, we see that we can use it to make sense of the very essential patterns and structures in the world.

You may notice that patterning is not well represented in current standards for the early childhood grades, and this is a concerning oversight. Young children need opportunities to recognize patterning in our world, create patterns of their own, and figure out how to extend those patterns. Research has shown that early exposure to patterns in nature, communities, art, and dance, among other areas, bolsters spatial reasoning, a key component of mathematical thinking (Hawes et al., 2017). In fact, when spatial reasoning develops, all forms of mathematical thinking grow, too, including counting, algebraic thinking, and relational thinking (Lowrie & Logan, 2018; Mix & Cheng, 2012). Patterning is clearly a big idea and deserves attention before, during, and after kindergarten (National Research Council, 2009).

Our Visualize activity invites students to first take the role of pattern seekers by sharing with them interesting photographs we have chosen that show different patterns. We ask students a critical question: What do you notice? and encourage them to discuss with each other, and you, the different patterns they see.

In our Play activity, students create their own patterns using a variety of different physical materials. We suggest that teachers work with students to recognize repeating patterns, and then have students work to make their own. As students physically handle blocks and also see patterns, they will be stimulating important brain connections.

In our Investigate activity, students experience opportunities for different brain activity by physically enacting a pattern through dance. Neuroscientist Sian Beilock has written an important book about the ways we learn through physical movement (*How the Body Knows Its Mind*, 2015) and highlights the important ways that mathematics is learned through movement. We bring movement to patterns by asking students to put animal movements together in a patterned way. Students can also invent different animal moves that they bring into a pattern, which they will enjoy very much!

Jo Boaler

References

Beilock, S. (2015). *How the body knows its mind: The surprising power of the physical environment to influence how you think and feel.* New York, NY: Simon & Schuster.

Devlin, K. (1994). *Mathematics, the science of patterns: The search for order in life, mind, and the universe.* New York, NY: Scientific American Library.

Hawes, Z., Moss, J., Caswell, B., Naqvi, S., & MacKinnon, S. (2017). Enhancing children's spatial and numerical skills through a dynamic spatial approach to early geometry instruction: Effects of a 32-week intervention. *Cognition and Instruction*, 35(3), 236–264.

Lowrie, T., & Logan, T. (2018) The interaction between spatial reasoning constructs and mathematics understandings in elementary classrooms. In K. Mix & M. Battista (Eds.), *Visualizing mathematics: The role of spatial reasoning in mathematical thought* (pp. 253–276). Heidelberg, Germany: Springer.

Mix, K. S., & Cheng, Y.-L. (2012). The relation between space and math: Developmental and educational implications. *Advances in Child Development and Behavior, 42*, 197–243.

National Research Council. (2009). *Mathematics learning in early childhood: Paths toward excellence and equity*. Washington, DC: The National Academies Press. https://doi.org/10.17226/12519

A World of Patterns

Snapshot

Students develop a working definition of *pattern* by looking for repetition in the real world, through photos and in the classroom and school.

Connection to CCSS
See Big Idea 7 "Introduction."

Agenda

Activity	Time	Description/Prompt	Materials
Launch	10 min	Show students the Checkerboard Tile image and ask what they notice. Use students' observations to name this as a *pattern*, something that repeats. Show students the Building Front image and tell them that it also contains patterns. Discuss the patterns that students can see in the image, pointing them out and saying them aloud.	• Checkerboard Tile sheet, to display • Building Front sheet, to display
Explore	15–30 min	Partners explore the classroom or school environment looking for patterns. Partners sketch and label each pattern they find, or capture it with a digital camera.	• Clipboard, paper, and colors, per partnership • Optional: digital camera, per partnership
Discuss	10 min	Share and discuss the patterns that students found in the classroom or school. For the patterns shared, support students in naming the pattern they see. Discuss how they know it is a pattern and whether it could be extended.	

Activity	Time	Description/Prompt	Materials
Extend	10–20 min	In a station or center, provide students with photos of patterns in the real world, along with colors. Students mark the photos to show the patterns they see.	• Images of patterns in the real world, such as the Elevators, Topiary Tree, Red Quilt, and Checkerboard Lawn sheets, one or more per student • Colors

To the Teacher

Patterning is a powerful mathematical idea and tool for understanding how our world is structured. Your students may or may not have encountered the term *pattern* before, but they have certainly seen patterns. In this activity, we connect the patterns students see all around them with the mathematical concept of patterning, using their experiences to develop a working definition of a pattern.

The pattern that students will most readily notice is an AB pattern (such as red-blue or square-circle), but we do not want to restrict students to just these types of patterns. Doing so can lead students to infer that all patterns are AB patterns. In this activity, we open up exploring for patterns to any that students can perceive and show. Before you begin this activity, you'll want to do a walk-through of your classroom or school spaces yourself to assess the kinds of patterns available to students. Look at the flooring, windows, light fixtures, doors, furniture, materials, books, bins, bulletin boards, and plants. What patterns might be most readily noticed by students? Which spaces in your building are the most pattern rich? Use your own observations to choose spaces for students to explore.

We have provided several additional images of pattern-rich spaces. We've suggested that you can use these in the extension for students to analyze and mark to show the patterns they see. Alternatively, you can use these images before sending students off to hunt for patterns in the real world, if you'd like students to have more experience looking for patterns in images first.

Activity

Launch

Launch the activity by showing students the Checkerboard Tile image on the document camera. Ask students, What do you notice? Give students a chance to turn and talk with a partner about what they see in the image. Take student observations, highlighting those that attend to the ways the squares are organized. Tell students that this is a *pattern*. Patterns repeat and can go on forever. Point to one edge of the image and ask students to predict what would be just off the edge. Invite students to share their ideas, and ask, How do you know? Point out the ways that students used the repetition in the pattern to make predictions about what would come next.

Show the Building Front image on the document camera, and tell students that there are patterns in this picture, too. Ask, What patterns do you see? Give students a chance to turn and talk to a partner. Take some observations and mark on the page the patterns that students see. Students may notice patterns in the windows, shapes, columns, shutters, or other decorations. Use words to make the repetition audible, such as repeating that a student saw "Short window, long window, short window. Short window, long window, short window."

Source: Shutterstock.com/t.natchai.

Explore

In partners, students go on a pattern hunt in your classroom or school. Provide each partnership with a clipboard and paper so that they can sketch and label the patterns they see. Alternatively, you could provide digital cameras, if they are available, for students to capture the patterns they see. Students should come back to the group ready to share their observations of patterns in the school.

These patterns can be based on colors, shapes, or objects. They can be found in the architecture, furniture, materials, or landscape design. For instance, students might notice patterns in the floor tiles, bins on classroom shelves, the arrangement of tables and chairs, or the doors and lights in the hallway. Although these patterns don't go on forever, they could be extended, and students could predict what would come next.

Discuss

Gather students together in a space where they can share the patterns they found, and discuss the following questions:

- What patterns did you find?
- How can we describe these patterns? (Support students in naming the pattern aloud, such as "Chair, chair, table. Chair, chair, table," or "Red, blue, red, blue, red, blue.")
- How do we know it is a pattern?
- What parts repeat? Do they repeat forever? Could they repeat forever?

Extend

In a station or center, provide students access to photos of the real world that contain patterns, such as those provided in this lesson. You can take your own pictures around the school or community, or draw on those that students took in this activity. Students, individually or in partners, write on the photos to show the patterns they see, using labels, colors, or other markings to show what parts they see repeating.

Look-Fors

- **Are students recognizing repetition as pattern?** Repetition can be hard for young students to see when what gets repeated is more than a single element. For instance, students will find repetition easy to see in a string of blue beads, but harder when that string is blue-red, with two elements alternating, and even more challenging if the beads repeat blue-red-green. The longer and more complex the repeated unit, the more difficult it will be for students to notice the structure. If you see that students are struggling to find patterns, you might ask, What do you see in this space/picture happening again and again? You might point students toward a direction for their eyes to travel, imagining that they encounter things on their way: What do you see again and again?
- **Are students attending to different properties to look for patterns?** For some students, the real challenge is decomposing the space to attend to elements that matter. For instance, students might not pay attention to the size of the bin on a shelf, but look only at their colors for patterns. Or perhaps color is irrelevant, and students need to pay attention to the furniture to see that chairs alternate with tables. Sorting out what to pay attention to and what to ignore may require some support. You might ask, If you only focus on color, do you see a pattern? If you only pay attention to shapes, do you see a pattern?

- **Can students predict the next element in a pattern?** One test for whether students have found a pattern is whether it could be extended, even if in the real world it actually ends. As you circulate while students look for patterns, ask students to describe the patterns they see, and ask, What would come next if the pattern kept going? How do you know? Students may not yet know how to extend the pattern, but you'll want to invite them to try. Often, making the pattern a verbal pattern can help students hear the rhythm and find the repetition. Encourage students to say their pattern aloud as a support for figuring out what might go next.

Reflect

What is a pattern?

Checkerboard Tile

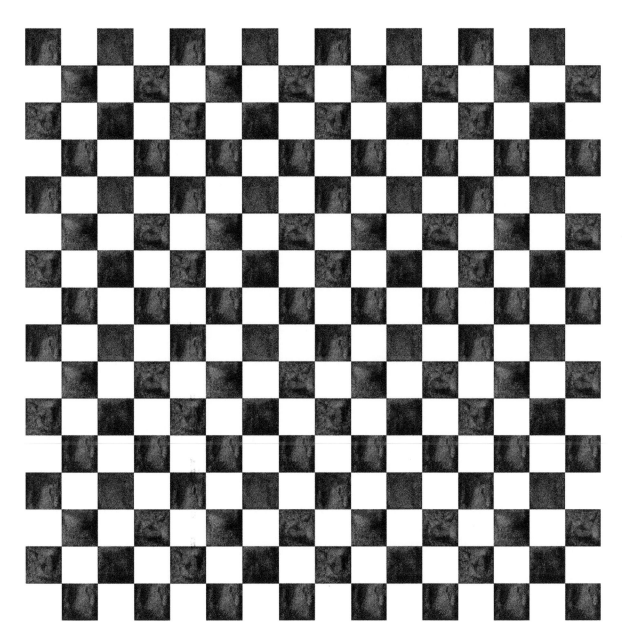

Elevators

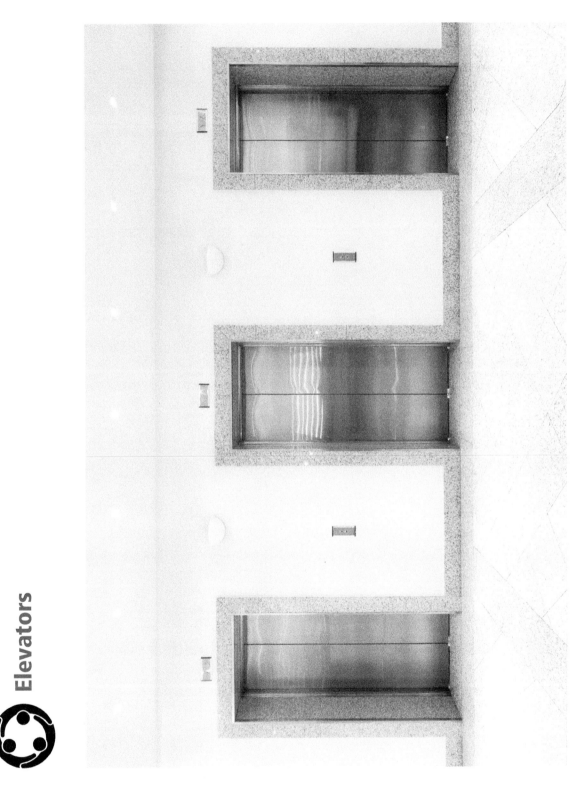

Topiary Trees

Red Quilt

Checkerboard Lawn

DIY Patterns

Snapshot

Students explore extending patterns through a pattern talk and then by creating their own using a variety of materials. The class discusses and compares the different patterns created.

Connection to CCSS
See Big Idea 7 "Introduction."

Agenda

Activity	Time	Description/Prompt	Materials
Launch	10 min	Show students an ABC pattern made with snap cubes and ask them what the pattern is. Come to agreement about what is repeating in the pattern. Ask students to predict what cube comes next in the pattern. Students offer and explain their answers. Once the class agrees, add that next cube to the pattern.	ABC pattern, repeated at least three times, made with snap cubes, to display
Play	20+ min	Partners choose a material and create their own patterns that extend as far as they would like. Leave patterns in place or take photos of them, before students move on to creating new patterns.	Make available: materials for pattern creation, such as snap cubes, square tiles, beads (and string or pipe cleaners), bears, coins, pattern blocks, or other small objects
Discuss	10 min	Invite students to share the patterns they have created, including similar patterns made out of different materials and any examples of complex patterns. Discuss what the pattern is, what could come next, and how it is similar to or different from other patterns that have been shared.	Partners' patterns to share

Activity	Time	Description/Prompt	Materials
Extend	15+ min	Make a patterning station or center where students can make patterns with a rotating set of materials. Students sketch or photograph their patterns and label the repeating parts.	Materials for pattern creation, such as snap cubes, square tiles, beads (and string or pipe cleaners), bears, coins, pattern blocks, or other small objects

To the Teacher

In this activity, we have designed the launch to resemble a dot or number talk. Instead of focusing on counting, these "pattern talks" invite students to predict what comes next by analyzing and extending the patterns you show. Just as with a dot talk, we encourage you to take student answers, ask for explanations, and support the class in coming to agreement. You can use this structure as a brief mathematical activity on any day, showing students part of a pattern and asking them to either describe the pattern or predict what comes next.

Students then play with designing and extending their own patterns using classroom objects. Make available to students objects such as snap cubes, tiles, chips, beads, bears, pattern blocks, or coins. You can offer any small objects that include some clear variation, such as in color or size, that can be used to build a pattern. Objects that are easier to pick up and array in a line are best.

Activity

Launch

Launch the activity by showing students an ABC pattern with snap cubes, such as red-blue-yellow, repeated at least three times.

ABC snap cube pattern: A = red, B = blue, C = yellow

Ask, What is the pattern? Give students a chance to turn and talk with a partner, and then take some ideas about the pattern. Be sure through this discussion that students see what parts repeat. Some students may come up and simply name all the colors they see, such as, "Red, blue, yellow, red, blue, yellow, red, blue, yellow." This is entirely appropriate and can help students hear the rhythm in pattern. You can ask students where they see the pattern beginning to repeat and break the stick of cubes to show the red-blue-yellow units. This may help some students perceive what is repeating.

Point to one end of the stick of cubes and ask, What cube makes sense to add next in this pattern? Give students a chance to turn and talk, and then take student ideas about what comes next in the pattern (either moving forward or backward) and press students to explain their reasoning. Come to agreement as a class about what comes next, and add that cube to the stick. You can repeat this process to build some momentum for extending patterns.

Play

Offer partners a choice of materials; each partnership should choose one type of material to work with to construct their own patterns. You might offer snap cubes, square tiles, beads (and string or pipe cleaners), bears, coins, pattern blocks, or other small objects.

Partners work together to make patterns from their objects. Students may want to extend their patterns very far—off the table, off the rug, out the room, down the hallway. As much as possible in your space, do not stop students as they are working to understand the idea that patterns really can go on forever. However, when students seem finished with one pattern, you can challenge them to create a new pattern. You can either have them keep their pattern where they have made it, or snap a photo of it so that you can save or share it. That way students can reuse the materials for the next pattern creation.

As you observe students creating patterns, ask, What's the pattern? How do you know? What comes next?

Discuss

Invite partners to share some of the patterns they created. You may want to select students in advance so that they can save these patterns for sharing. Select students who have made the same pattern (e.g., AB) out of different materials so that students can compare these to see how they are similar even when made from different materials. Also select some more complex patterns to share, if you notice anyone making AAB, ABC, AABB, or something more elaborate. For each pattern shared, discuss the following questions:

- What is the pattern? How do you know?
- What would come next in the pattern? How do you know?
- How is this like (or different from) other patterns we've seen?

Extend

Make a patterning station or center, where students can work with a rotating set of materials to create new patterns. Students can then draw or photograph their pattern creations and label them to show what parts repeat. You can use these photos as a resource for additional pattern talks with the class.

Look-Fors

- **Are students constructing patterns?** Constructing patterns is challenging work, and you'll want to pay attention to whether students have a clear repeating structure to their string of objects. Ask students to describe the pattern to you. Ask, What part repeats? Support students in showing you how their pattern repeats. You might ask them to put their hand or fingers on the objects that repeat, showing how these parts repeat along the string. If you notice that students are making nonrepeating strings of objects, you might ask, What is a pattern? Or consider showing students the snap-cube pattern you used in the launch and asking them to tell what makes it a pattern. You can then ask, How can you make your objects into a pattern?

- **Are students using a small set of items (A and B, or A, B, and C) for patterning?** If students have available to them a set of objects with many different types, they may be tempted to use all of them in constructing a pattern, perhaps getting lost in the complexity. For instance, students using pattern blocks, which have six shapes and colors, might try to use all six and not be able yet to hold a pattern with so many elements. If you see this, say something like, "I see you are using lots of different shapes (or colors) in your pattern, and it is a little hard to see what repeats. Can you choose two or three types of pieces to use to make a pattern?" Once students have selected the components they want to work with, you can ask, What pattern can you make with those?

- **Are students holding the pattern?** Just as we find that one-to-one correspondence can break down, students may be able to start a pattern but not continue it beyond some point. For instance, you may see students who start a pattern green-green-red, green-green-red, green-green-red, that at some point becomes green-red-red. You might draw students' attention to where the pattern changes by explicitly saying, "It looks like your pattern changed here." Or you can ask students to locate the change, by asking, Can you tell where your pattern changed? Fixing a pattern with a mistake is conceptually very challenging. Invite students to try, but if they become stuck, invite them instead to try making a new pattern. Ask them to focus on keeping the pattern the same as they build a new one.

- **How long do students want their patterns to be before they feel finished?** As stated earlier, some students may want to build their patterns very long, beyond the bounds of a table or even the classroom. When students are doing this, two key ideas are at work. First, students are working on holding their pattern over a great number of repetitions. Second, students are testing the bounds of the infinite. If we tell students that a pattern can go on forever, we are inviting them to explore this idea. Students may be asking themselves, Can it *really* go on *forever*? Obviously, there are limits to the space, time, and materials available, but to the extent possible, allow students to test the notion of forever, rather than ushering them off to a new pattern. By contrast, some students may make a pattern, get to the edge of the table, and decide they are done. Allow them to start again, but you may want to press their ideas about forever by asking, If the table were bigger, could the pattern keep going? How far? How do you know?

Reflect

How do you make a pattern?

Kinder Dance Party

Snapshot

Students investigate how they can embody patterns by creating and teaching patterned animal dances.

Connection to CCSS
See Big Idea 7.

Agenda

Activity	Time	Description/Prompt	Materials
Launch	10 min	Teach students two animal movements, and then put them together to make a patterned dance, such as AAB or AABB. Record this dance using symbols on a chart, and practice as a class. Teach students one more animal move and together design a new dance that includes that move and one or both of the originals. Practice this dance together.	• Chart and markers • Optional: music
Explore	15–20 min	Partners invent animal dance moves and assemble them into a patterned dance. Partners practice their dance until they feel they could teach it to someone else. You may want to pair up partnerships for them to try teaching their dance to others and learning a new dance from them.	
Discuss	15 min	Invite some partnerships to teach their dance moves and patterned dances to the class. Record each dance using symbols on a chart. Discuss what the different dances have in common and what makes them different. Partners share how they designed their dances.	• Chart and markers • Optional: music

Activity	Time	Description/Prompt	Materials
Extend	30+ min	Introduce sounds, such as clapping or stomping, as new tools for creating patterned dances or songs. Partners can combine movements and sounds to create new patterns.	• Recording tools, such as paper and colors • Optional: tools for making sounds, such as drums, sticks, and rattles

To the Teacher

This activity is based on the work of Tom Lowrie and his team at Early Learning STEM Australia (ELSA) who have been investigating how to embed patterning concepts into preschool and kindergarten classrooms in that country for many years. In this activity, we invite students to investigate how to use simple animal motions to develop patterned dances; patterns are something they can embody, not just make with materials. This embodied cognition, which involves using both sides of the body to produce movements, encourages the development of connections across both sides of the brain and between the body and cognition.

We have created some examples of animals and matching dance moves, but we encourage you to develop your own, tailoring them to the animals children might encounter in your community or those that your students are particularly interested in. The following are some possible moves you could introduce to children:

- Rabbit (or frog): hop
- Chick: flap wings
- Alligator: extend arms like a mouth and snap them shut
- Snake: wiggle
- Fish: put hands together and swim them forward
- Cat: pounce forward with fingers like claws

You want the animals to be familiar and interesting, and the associated moves to be simple to be in keeping with kindergarten gross motor capacity. During these dances, you can play simple music in the background to give the dance a rhythm.

We encourage you to consider extending this activity by including an exploration of dances more broadly. Most dances are patterned, particularly traditional dances. Consider how you could make connections in your local community by inviting others in to teach students patterned dances.

Activity

Launch

Launch the activity by telling students that they are going to be doing some pattern dances, making patterns with their bodies. Introduce students to two animal moves, such as those described in the To the Teacher section, and practice these moves together until students feel comfortable with each. Then create a short pattern dance with the two moves. We recommend an AAB or AABB pattern, such as chick-chick-snake. Show your dance on a chart with images for the two moves.

Teacher-created class display of the chick-chick-snake dance

Practice the dance as a class and be sure to go through several repetitions. You may want to play music as students dance. As you do each move, say the animal name aloud, such as "Chick, chick, snake."

Show students one more move and invite the class to design a new dance that uses this move with one or both of the original two. Design a dance together, adding it to your chart. Practice the dance as a class. You might ask, How many moves are in our dance before it repeats?

Explore

In partners, students design a patterned dance. They can use the animal moves you have taught them or invent their own. You can imagine there will be students who want to create a dance like T-rex–T-rex–velociraptor. Partners design the moves and the dance, practicing the dance so that they are ready to teach others.

You may want to pair up groups to teach one another their moves, practicing one another's dances and how to teach their moves to others. If you choose to try this, each group will have the opportunity to share and teach their dance to someone else.

Discuss

Invite some groups to teach their pattern dances to the class. Students will need to show and explain their moves first, and then teach the pattern dance. On a chart, draw symbols for the parts of each dance the class learns so they can refer back to these as the class dances together. Be sure to say the animal names aloud with each movement.

After the class has learned a couple of dances, you might use the chart you have created to discuss the following questions:

- What makes these dances similar?
- What makes these dances different?
- How did you decide how to design your dance? What is the pattern?

Extend

Introduce the class to musical elements that students can combine into dances and songs, such as claps, stomps, tapping two sticks together, shaking a rattle, ringing bells, or slapping a drum. Students can design patterned dances or songs with moves and sounds mixed. You may want to move this activity to a larger space or outside to help students pay attention to their own sounds. Provide students with a tool for recording their patterns with symbols, just as you have done on the chart. These will help them remember and communicate their dances or songs to others. Invite students to teach their patterned dances or songs to the class. Consider hosting a performance of students' patterned dances and songs for families or other classes.

Look-Fors

- **Are students defining their moves clearly?** One of the challenges of creating patterned movements is that, unlike pattern blocks or snap cubes, they are not preconstructed objects to select. Students must either remember motions you taught them (such as chick and snake) or create their own to serve as building blocks for a dance. Making these motions "animals" supports students in thinking of each motion as a unit that they can name, use, and replicate. Ask students, What animals are in your dance? Can you show me the motion for each one? Look for partners to have agreement on both the name of the animal and the associated movement. If you notice a significant difference, draw students' attention to this by saying something like, "I see that you are each doing different things for 'alligator.' Which is it?" If partners don't agree on the motion, they will struggle to teach others.

- **Are students creating a brief string of repeatable movements?** Once students have clear movements, they need to create a short string that can be repeated. Ask students to share their dances with you, even if they are still figuring out what that dance might be. Notice whether students are focusing on defining the repeatable core unit of the dance, or just stringing different movements together with no repetition in sight. Ask, What part of your dance gets repeated? Watch students to see whether they are being consistent with repeating the core unit. As in the Play activity, students may understand the need to repeat and begin consistently, but at some point lose the pattern. Just invite them to restart and see whether they can keep the rhythm. If it is truly too challenging, you can ask students whether it makes sense to simplify their pattern. For instance, students who create an AABCBC pattern may find this far too complex to hold, but AABC or ABC may be more memorable.

- **Do students notice that the pattern can be the same even if the moves used are different?** In your discussion, draw attention to any patterns that are the same, such as those that are AAB like the chick-chick-snake dance the class performed in the launch. Ask students what these dances have in common and see whether they notice that they involve the same structure, even when the animal moves themselves are different. You may want to name these using letters (such as AAB) to highlight the connection. Students do not need this language, but it may help them see connections between patterns. Similarly, the chart you created with the symbols for each dance can be cut into strips so that patterns with the same structure can be arrayed one on top of the other to help students see the connections.

Reflect

How are dances also patterns?

Stretching Counting toward 100

In Big Idea 5, I talked about the importance of number flexibility. In this big idea, we take number flexibility to the next level with higher numbers that we know students will be excited to encounter. My experience of young students tells me that they are fascinated by the idea of numbers that are big, and even ideas about infinity. We ask students to think of 100 made up of objects of different sizes, continuing to keep ideas of number as visuals and objects, enabling connections to be made between different areas of the brain. This big idea also contains demands of organization, which is an idea that pervades all of mathematics. In my teaching of middle-school students, I have found that something that separates higher- from lower-achieving students is their capacity to keep ideas in an organized way. Often we do not teach students to organize well, but just assume that they will be able to. This big idea requires students to organize their thinking, to make conjectures about their thinking, and to display their organizations, all of which provide timely teaching moments. As students approach numbers with flexibility, group and sort objects, organize their thinking, make conjectures, and visualize numbers, they will be engaging in a range of mathematical acts that are essential to the modern world.

In our Visualize activity, students return to counting collections, now developing strategies for organizing objects to count much larger collections. This is an act of organization that is good to focus on and help students with. Students are shown a large collection of objects and asked how they could count them and what strategies they might use to figure out how many there are, keeping careful records as they go. We suggest that you make the counting of large collections an ongoing activity, giving students many opportunities to estimate sizes and to choose and count collections of different sizes.

In our Play activity, students organize 20 items from a collection, with the intent of expressing a way to quantify objects without counting each item one by one. Students learn to think about ways to organize their collection so that it is possible to see how many objects there are in total. In this activity, students need to use their number flexibility with numbers up to 20, bringing in the teen numbers. This is an important cognitive development and one that should be accompanied by number flexibility as students learn to see and make sense of patterns that are similar to the ones they developed for 1–10.

In our Investigate activity, students get to play with an object that can be a wonderful playground of patterns—the hundred chart. Your students probably know 1 to 10 very well now and can be introduced to a larger set of numbers that they can explore with flexibility. They will be able to find patterns and think about what they mean. I love the questions for students: What do you notice? What do you wonder? Give students time to explore patterns and make conjectures. We have included a blank row at the end so that students can think about what comes next!

Jo Boaler

Counting Larger Collections

Snapshot

Students return to counting collections, now developing strategies for organizing objects to count much larger collections.

Connection to CCSS
K.CC.5, K.CC.1

Agenda

Activity	Time	Description/Prompt	Materials
Launch	5–10 min	Show students a large collection of objects and ask them how they would count the objects to figure out how many there are. Invite students to show how they could get started, and highlight any strategies that organize the objects. Tell students that they will be counting a large collection and should pay attention to ways to organize to keep track.	Large collection of objects, such as snap cubes or coins
Explore	30+ min	Partners count a large collection of objects, working on ways to organize the objects to keep track of the count. Partners record their count and leave it with the collection. Students can then swap with another group to check their count, coming together to discuss if they disagree.	• Collection of 30–200 objects, per partnership • Make available: containers for grouping objects, such as cups or bowls • Recording tools, such as paper, index cards, clipboards, and pencils

Activity	Time	Description/Prompt	Materials
Discuss	10–15 min	Invite students who developed organization strategies for counting their objects to share these with the class. Discuss why these are helpful. Discuss any disagreements that arose during the counting process and how students resolved these.	
Extend	Ongoing	Make counting large collections an ongoing activity, in which students choose and count collections of different sizes and compare their counts to those of others. Extend students' thinking by asking them to estimate the number of objects in the collection before counting and then comparing their estimates to the actual count.	• Collection of 30–200 objects, per partnership • Make available: containers for grouping objects, such as cups or bowls • Recording tools, such as paper, index cards, clipboards, and pencils

To the Teacher

In this activity, we are circling back to the work of counting collections from the first big idea. Students need extended opportunities to count increasingly large collections of objects to develop ideas about the quantity that different numbers represent, how numbers are organized, and how to organize objects to count them. Counting objects supports students in extending their one-to-one correspondence capacity toward 100, matching the oral counting sequence to objects. As they count collections, students begin to build references for how much quantities actually are. For instance, how big is 28? What does it look like? What does 28 blocks look like? How does 28 look different if you are counting coins or bears?

We encourage you to make counting collections an ongoing and central activity in your kindergarten math classroom. In this activity, we offer ideas about how you can continue this work with larger collections, and we highly recommend Franke, Kazemi, and Turrou's (2018) book on the topic for a more in-depth examination. You will need several large collections of objects, particularly objects that are easy to arrange without their falling or rolling away. Collections should be matched to the numbers that students are ready to work with. You may have some students working hard on counting in the teen numbers, while others are pushing toward and beyond 100. Point partners toward collections they are ready to tackle, knowing that these will and should change over time. Everyday objects are typically the most convenient and useful for collections, including classroom manipulatives (such as cubes, tiles, or pattern blocks), bins of books, school supplies, and coins.

Activity

Launch

Launch the activity by showing students a large collection of at least 100 objects. You might choose a collection that students encounter in your class every day, such as a bin of snap cubes, or something new, such as a jar of coins. Ask, How would you count these objects to figure out how many we have? Give students a chance to turn and talk to a neighbor. Invite students to come up and show some of the ways they might get started on their counting. Point out any strategies you see students using to organize for counting, such as moving objects, lining them up, or making groups. Tell students that these strategies can be useful for keeping track of the objects they're counting.

Tell students that they are going to work on strategies for counting larger collections than they have before. Ask students to pay attention to how they are organizing their objects to count so that they don't lose track.

Explore

Provide each partnership with a large collection of objects. These collections can vary from 30 to 200 objects, depending on what you think each partnership might be ready for. Partners work together to count how many objects are in their collection and to record their count in some way on paper. As you circulate while students count, press them to organize for counting. This might involve lining up objects or forming groups. Make available containers that students might use to make groups, such as cups, bowls, or muffin tins.

Once a partnership is confident in their count of the collection, ask them to try a new collection by swapping with another group. Each group can leave a record of their count with the collection, and the next group can check the count. If groups disagree, bring them together to discuss and recount.

Discuss

As you observe students counting, select one or more groups to share something about their counting, particularly challenges they faced or strategies they developed for organizing, such as grouping. These students do not need to recount all of their objects in front of the class; rather, they can share the strategies or challenges, regardless of whether or not they completed their count or overcame their struggles. Discuss the following questions:

- How can we organize our objects to help us see how many or keep track?
- Did you have any disagreements? How did you figure out what the count was when you disagreed?

Draw particular attention to the ways that students are beginning to use grouping, whether they are simply counting by touch two objects at a time or putting objects in cups in groups of 5 or 10 (or any other increment). Some organizing strategies are helpful for ensuring that all objects get counted, such as lining the objects up. Other strategies support students in counting the total without losing track, or allow students to use skip counting as a tool. Be sure to highlight the utility of the different strategies your students developed.

Extend

In keeping with the work of Franke et al. (2018), we see counting collections of objects as ongoing work across weeks. While continuing to count larger collections, you might extend students' thinking by asking them to estimate the number of objects in their collection before counting and to record their estimate on a card. Encourage students to use references in the classroom, such as other collections that have already been counted and labeled, to develop their estimates.

Partners then count their collections, and then they can record the actual amount in the collection. Ask, Was your estimate close? Was it too high or too low? How do you know? Use this to help students develop some ideas about estimating quantity and making comparisons between numbers.

Look-Fors

- **What numbers are students ready to count?** You will have likely observed students counting throughout the year and have a sense of the horizon of students' counting capacities. When you watch students count collections, you'll want to be looking for a few key indicators that will help you stretch that capacity without frustrating students. First, look for students' one-to-one correspondence, and be sure to attend to both partners in any group. At what point does one-to-one correspondence break down, if at all? You'll want to provide students with collections that are up to this point and just a little beyond so that they have opportunities to grow. Second, listen to the counting sequence itself. Students may have one number name for each object, but use an unconventional sequence, such as 13, 14, 16, 18, which leads to an inaccurate total count of the collection. You do not need to use this as a way to limit the size of the collection, unless students are stuck in a circular counting sequence, such as 20, 21, 22, . . . 29, 20, 21, 22, . . . Third, look for the ways that students organize for counting. If students are counting smaller collections successfully without moving the objects as they count or lining them up, you may want to increase the size of the collection to create motivation for developing organizing strategies.

- **How are students developing grouping strategies?** One of the central goals of counting larger collections is to encourage students to develop grouping strategies. Grouping strategies form the basis for understanding place value, the way that we group numbers into 10s and 1s. Students are likely to begin grouping by trying much smaller groups, sometimes just in pairs, or in groups that older students would see as difficult to count, such as groups of threes or fours. The development of any grouping strategy moves students conceptually toward place value and should be encouraged. As students develop more sophisticated counting strategies, they may match those with grouping strategies. That is, when students learn how to count by 2s, they may group by 2s; conversely, grouping by 2s can support students in learning to skip-count by 2s. If you see students beginning to cluster objects, offer them tools that might be supportive, such as cups or bowls. Ask, How did you decide that groups would be helpful? How big are your groups? Why did you choose that size for your groups?

- **Are you beginning to see skip counting?** Grouping strategies and the development of skip counting are closely related. As mentioned earlier, grouping objects gives students a reason to skip-count, and knowing how to skip-count makes grouping useful. Listen for students using skip counting with their groups. At an early stage, you may hear students subvocalize some of the counting as they learn a particular skip-counting pattern, counting some numbers softly under their breath and then the final member of the group aloud. This can sound like, "One, TWO, three, FOUR, five, SIX, . . ." when counting by 2s, or "One, two, THREE, four, five, SIX, . . ." when counting by 3s. Later, you may hear full skip counting: "2, 4, 6, 8, . . ." Be sure to have students share the work they are doing to count the groups they have made and how skip counting can make counting groups easier. If you know students have been working on skip counting by 2s or 5s, you might ask them how they could use that to help count their objects, encouraging grouping strategies.

Reflect

What do you have to do differently to count a very large collection?

Reference

Franke, M. L., Kazemi, E., & Turrou, A. C. (2018). *Choral counting & counting collections*. Portsmouth, NH: Stenhouse.

BIG IDEA 8: STRETCHING COUNTING TOWARD 100

Making a Collection

Snapshot

Students make collections with a particular number of objects in the set, developing ways to organize and display the collection to make it easier for others to count.

Connection to CCSS
K.CC.5, K.CC.4, K.CC.1, K.CC.3, K.NBT.1

Agenda

Activity	Time	Description/Prompt	Materials
Launch	10 min	Show students a container of 20 blocks and tell them that there are 20 blocks inside. Ask, How can we organize these to show that there are 20? Take student ideas and invite them to show how they might organize the objects.	Container of 20 blocks or other small manipulative
Play	20 min	Give each partnership a target number for building a collection. Partners construct and organize a collection to make it easier to see how many objects it contains. Groups trade places and examine the ways that others have organized their collections, checking their counts.	• Sticky note or index card with a number for each group • Make available: objects for making collections, such as snap cubes, blocks, chips, or square tiles, and tools for organizing, such as cups or bowls
Discuss	10 min	Discuss the ways that students organized their collections and which ways made it easier to see or count how many objects the collection contained.	Optional: chart and markers

Activity	Time	Description/Prompt	Materials
Extend	20–30 min	Make a station or center in which partners count and organize a collection with a target number of objects. Students draw and label their ways of organizing the collection. Post these for others to see as they visit the station. Discuss the different ways students organized and recorded the same quantity.	• Objects for making a collection, such as snap cubes or square tiles • Posted target number • Recording tools, such as paper and pencils

To the Teacher

In this activity, we build on the work students have done counting collections, moving here to constructing and organizing collections of objects. Constructing a set of a particular quantity requires a slightly different use of counting than does counting a given set. Students need to keep in mind the target quantity as they are counting and notice its relationship to the counting sequence so that they can decide when to stop. Many students will likely get into a counting rhythm and go past the target quantity, only to notice at some point that they have forgotten what the goal was. Students will likely need to count and recount to be certain they have the target number of objects in their collection.

We suggest that you choose this target number for each partnership based on your observations during the Visualize activity. You want the target number to be a quantity large enough that students can reliably count, rather than a number that stretches their counting capacity. For instance, if you have a pair of students who began to struggle counting a collection of objects at 29, then you may want to choose a target number of 25 objects for that group.

The key idea in this activity is to promote organizing quantities in ways that make it easier to see and count the number of objects in the set, particularly by grouping. Students may group objects into groups of 2, 3, 4, 5, or 10. Students may select groups that they know how to skip-count by, or not. Students may cluster objects together (such as by placing five cubes in a cup) or arrange them so they are easier to see (such as by arranging square tiles in columns of five). Be sure to notice the different features of their organizing and ask questions about how these different ways make it easier to see or check the count.

When selecting materials for this activity, we suggest a narrower selection than in the Visualize activity. Provide materials that support organization, such as snap cubes, square tiles, or blocks. These materials can be joined or arranged in clear rows, columns, or rectangles.

Activity

Launch

Launch the activity by showing the class a collection of 20 blocks or other small manipulatives in a container. Tell students that there are 20 objects in the container. Ask, How can we organize these to show that there are 20 objects? Give students a chance to turn and talk to a partner. Invite students to come show how they might organize the objects. You may want the class in a circle so that you can dump all the objects in the center where everyone can see different ideas for how to organize them. Point out that there are different ways to do this, and today their goal is to try to display their collections so that others can count it more easily.

Play

Assign each partnership a number on a sticky note or index card, and ask them to make a collection with this number of objects in it. Draw on your observations of their counting in the Visualize activity to select a number that students will feel confident counting. Provide access to small objects for constructing a collection, such as snap cubes, blocks, chips, or tiles, and tools for organizing, such as cups or bowls.

Once students have constructed a collection of the target number of objects, partners work together to organize their collection so that someone else can more easily count it, whatever that means to them. Students may construct groups or array the objects in lines or other shapes.

When partners are satisfied with their organization, have them place their number (on the sticky note or index card you provided) by their collection. Then invite them to switch places with another group and examine how the other group organized their collection. Students explore the following questions:

- How did they organize their collection?
- How can you use that organization to help you check their count?
- Do you agree with their count? Why or why not?

Ask students to leave their organized collections out, so that you can show them to others during the discussion. You may want to get students up to look or take a picture to project for all to see. Gather students to discuss the following questions:

- How did you organize your collection so that others could more easily count it?
- How did you count others' collections?
- Which ways of organizing made it easiest to check the count?

Name these methods for organizing quantities, either by their mathematical names (e.g., "groups of 5") or by the students who invented it (e.g., "Jose and Jessinia's way is groups of 5"). You may want to make a chart of these methods, drawing pictures so that students can see the different ways.

Extend

Create a station or center for students to organize collections of objects in different ways. Provide students with a group of small objects that are easy to organize, such as snap cubes or square tiles, and a target number for the collection. Choose a target number that introduces multiple ways that students might organize using groups, such as a multiple of 10 or 5. Partners work together to count and organize a collection of the objects matching the target number. Students draw and label a picture to show the ways that they organized the collection. Post these in the area of the center so that others can use them to get ideas for ways to organize the collection. After several days, discuss the following questions about how students organized the same quantity differently:

- How did you organize your collection so that we could see the number of objects?
- Which ways of organizing do we think are most helpful? Why?
- Did anyone try out a new way of organizing? What did you try?
- How did you record your ways of organizing?

Look-Fors

- **Do students have an understanding of what it means to organize for counting?** Organization as a concept may be new for students and can have multiple meanings. For instance, in an everyday sense, we may use the word *organize* to mean "neaten," "put away," or "sort" rather than "create systematic order." During the launch, you'll want to make sure that students get some ideas from one another about what it means to organize a collection for counting. For instance, when we are counting a collection, variation in the objects isn't relevant, and there is no real need to sort the objects by color, for example, to facilitate counting. Instead, organizing for counting means creating a different kind of order, in which quantity, groups, and arrangements are the focus. During the launch and then later while you observe students working, look for evidence that students understand the idea of organizing for counting, such as making groups or arrays, or lining up objects. Students who do not yet understand this idea may sort by color or build pictures with their objects. You might ask, How can you arrange the objects on your table to make them easier to count?

- **Are students using grouping strategies to organize?** Grouping strategies move students closer to understanding how our number system is organized through place value. Even when students use groups other than 10s and 1s, they are moving toward this idea. Look for the diverse ways that students group, including different-size groups and different ways to arrange those groups. Groups may be organized themselves, such as columns of snap cubes, or not, such as cups of cubes. During the discussion, you'll want to highlight these differences. One key feature to attend to is whether students who are using grouping are doing so consistently. For example, you may notice a partnership using cups to organize their collection, but the cups each have different numbers of objects. You might say something like, "I notice that you're making groups. Groups can be really helpful for counting. How are you deciding how many go in each group?" Encourage students to think about how groups of equal size can be more useful for counting. Students may need to make unequal groups and try to count them before noticing that equal groups are more useful. This, also, can be a helpful process to share during the discussion.

- **Are students using the organization of objects to support counting?** When students recount their own collections or those made by others, you'll want to attend to whether students are using the organizational system to support counting. For instance, you may see students simply counting the collection one by one regardless of how the objects are arranged. Ask, How are these objects organized? How could you use that to help you count? For some students, the organizational system may not support counting. For instance, if the objects are organized into groups of three, students are unlikely to know how to skip-count by 3s and instead will count by 1s. This is something to share during the discussion as the class identifies that some ways of organizing are more helpful for counting than others.

Reflect

How can organizing help us see *how many*?

Hundred Chart Patterns

Snapshot

Students investigate patterns in the hundred chart, exploring how our number system is organized.

Agenda

Activity	Time	Description/Prompt	Materials
Launch	5–10 min	Show students the hundred chart and ask, How is this organized? What patterns do you see? Take a few student ideas and show how they could record two of these using different colors on the hundred chart.	• Hundred Chart sheet, to display • Colors
Explore	20+ min	Partners investigate the patterns on the hundred chart, recording each using color and a label on the Hundred Chart sheet. Partners look for as many patterns as they can find.	• Hundred Chart sheet, multiple per partnership • Colors, per partnership
Discuss	15 min	Discuss and share the patterns that students found and how they recorded them on the Hundred Chart sheets. Introduce language, as needed, to describe these patterns. Point out the empty boxes at the bottom and ask students to predict the numbers that come next. Discuss whether these follow the patterns students found.	Optional: Hundred Chart sheet, to display, and colors

Activity	Time	Description/Prompt	Materials
Extend	15+ min	In a station or center, show students the Hundred Chart Puzzles and explain that some of the numbers are missing. Ask, How can you use the patterns in the hundred chart to find what numbers are missing? After students have had a chance to explore one or more puzzles, discuss the strategies they developed and how they used patterns to find the missing numbers.	Hundred Chart Puzzles, multiple of each

To the Teacher

This investigation offers kindergarten students nearing the end of the year the opportunity to stretch their connections between counting and written numbers by looking for patterns in the hundred chart. The hundred chart contains a seemingly endless number of patterns. Students can and will continue to explore these for many years, developing their understanding of the counting sequence, place value, skip counting, factors and multiples, and properties of number. This investigation is just a first exploration of the patterns students might see, and the first time we are inviting students to consider patterns numerically.

Students may notice a wide variety of numerical patterns in the hundred chart, and we encourage you to be open to many different interpretations of what could constitute a pattern. Some patterns students may notice include the following:

- Smaller numbers are at the top, and bigger numbers are at the bottom.
- Numbers at the top have only one digit, most of the numbers have two digits, and there is one at the bottom with three digits.
- Decade numbers, or numbers ending with zero, are in a column on the right.
- Each column of numbers ends with the same digit (in the 1s place).
- All the 20s are in a row, except for 20 (and similarly for other decades).

You'll want to make sure that students see overall patterns (such as smallest numbers at the top), vertical patterns (such as the decade numbers in the right-most column), and horizontal patterns (such as the 10s being the same until the final number in each row).

We invite students to use different colors to color in the patterns they notice. Color coding like this is likely to be new, and some students may prefer to show each pattern on a different hundred grid for greater clarity. What is important is that students can show, track, and share the patterns they notice. Provide students with access to as many colors and hundred grids as they need to notice and record patterns for sharing.

Noticing all the 1s

Counting by 2s

Activity

Launch

Launch the activity by showing students the hundred chart on the document camera, and tell students that this tool is called a *hundred chart*. Ask, How is this organized? What patterns do you see? Give students a chance to turn and talk with a partner. Invite students to share a few ideas to get their thinking going. Choosing two of the patterns that students shared, point out how they show the patterns with different colors on the hundred chart.

Explore

Provide partners with Hundred Chart sheets and colors. Partners explore the question, What patterns are in the hundred chart? For each pattern that partners find, they color the chart to show the pattern for others to see. Encourage students to label their patterns in some way. Students try to find as many patterns as they can, recording each in a different color on the same sheet or on different sheets.

Discuss

Gather students together to share the patterns they found and discuss the following questions:

- What patterns did you notice in the chart?
- How can we describe those patterns? (Offer students language to help them articulate what they have noticed.)
- How did you show those patterns on the chart?

Be sure that students have the chance to share how they recorded the patterns on their own sheets. You may also want to record these patterns on a class Hundred Chart sheet. However, if students have noticed a lot of patterns, collecting these all onto one sheet can be overwhelming visually. Using multiple sheets or students' own sheet may be more effective for showing the patterns. We encourage you to find a space to post these patterns as a reference for future exploration, including the extension that follows.

Once students have shared all the patterns they have found, point out the empty row of boxes at the bottom of the hundred chart. Ask, What do you think comes next in the chart? Discuss what numbers come next and how you might record them. Ask, Do these follow the patterns you found? Why or why not?

Extend

In a station or center, introduce students to the Hundred Chart Puzzles. Show students that there are two kinds of puzzles that they can solve with a partner. In one kind of puzzle, you can see the entire hundred chart, but some of the numbers are missing. In another kind of puzzle, you can only see part of the hundred chart, and, again, some of the numbers are missing. Ask, How can you use the patterns in the hundred chart to find what numbers are missing?

Provide students access to multiple puzzles and, if you have posted the patterns students found in the hundred chart, you might remind students that they can use these as a reference. After students have had a chance to explore one or more puzzles, discuss the strategies students used to figure out what number might be missing in each blank spot.

Look-Fors

- **What language do students need in order to name the patterns they see?** There are many words that may be useful for describing the patterns in the hundred chart that students may not have had the need to know until now.

Take advantage of this opportunity to provide the language that students need in order to communicate their observations with increasing precision. Students may benefit from words such as *vertical, horizontal, column, row*, and *digit* when describing the patterns they see. Students may also need positional terms to describe the relationship between different numbers, such as *on top of, above, below, next to, left*, and *right*.

- **Do students notice patterns vertically and horizontally?** By having students examine patterns in the hundred chart, we aim to open up conversations that have been developing through counting collections of objects. Among the many patterns in the hundred chart are those connected to place value. Reading the chart vertically, we want students to notice that the 1s, or last, digit remains the same, while the number of 10s keeps going up: 6, 16, 26, 36, 46, 56, . . . Reading the chart horizontally, we want students to notice a nearly inverted pattern. The number of 10s remains the same until the very end of the row, but the number of 1s continues to count up, one by one: 21, 22, 23, 24, 25, 26, . . . Each of these patterns requires that students attend to what is happening to each of the digits and notice that different patterns emerge. Students may not yet understand what is driving these patterns, but noticing them is the first step to making sense of them.

- **Are students thinking about what happens on the chart through movement?** One way to look for patterns is to ask, What happens to the numbers when I move in a particular way? This can be applied to the vertical and horizontal patterns discussed earlier. For instance, students might ask themselves, What happens to the numbers when I move across this row? Other forms of movement are possible, too. For instance, What happens when I move down and across, like on a set of stairs? What happens when I move up instead of down? For students who are uncertain about how to proceed or those who have exhausted the patterns they notice, encourage them to think about movement in searching for patterns.

- **Does anyone see skip-counting patterns?** Beyond patterns that make up entire columns or rows, there are many interesting patterns in the hundred chart that come from skip counting. If students skip-count by increments they are comfortable with, such as 2s, 5s, or 10s, they will find additional patterns. Patterns grow more complex if students skip-count by other numbers, such as 3s, 4s, or 6s. Engaging with skip counting is not something that all children will choose to do. But if you notice students creating patterns on the chart through patterned counting, ask questions about what they are trying and be sure that students have a chance to share it with the class.

Reflect

What was the most interesting pattern in the hundred chart? Why?

Hundred Chart

1	2	3	4	5	6	7	8	9	10
11	12	13	14	15	16	17	18	19	20
21	22	23	24	25	26	27	28	29	30
31	32	33	34	35	36	37	38	39	40
41	42	43	44	45	46	47	48	49	50
51	52	53	54	55	56	57	58	59	60
61	62	63	64	65	66	67	68	69	70
71	72	73	74	75	76	77	78	79	80
81	82	83	84	85	86	87	88	89	90
91	92	93	94	95	96	97	98	99	100

Hundred Chart Puzzle 1

1	2	3	4	5	6	7	8	9	10
11	12	13	14	15	16	17	18	19	20
21	22	23	24	25	26	27	28	29	30
31	32	33	34	35	36	37	38	39	40
51	52	53	54	55	56	57	58	59	60
61	62	63	64	65	66	67	68	69	70
71	72	73	74	75	76	77	78	79	80
81	82	83	84	85	86	87	88	89	90
91	92	93	94	95	96	97	98	99	100

Hundred Chart Puzzle 2

1	2	3	4	5	6	7		9	10
11	12	13	14	15	16	17		19	20
21	22	23	24	25	26	27		29	30
31	32	33	34	35	36	37		39	40
41	42	43	44	45	46	47		49	50
51	52	53	54	55	56	57		59	60
61	62	63	64	65	66	67		69	70
71	72	73	74	75	76	77		79	80
81	82	83	84	85	86	87		89	90
91	92	93	94	95	96	97		99	100

Hundred Chart Puzzle 3

1	2	3	4	5
	12	13	14	15
21		23	24	25
31	32	33	34	35
41	42	43		45
51	52	53	54	

Hundred Chart Puzzle 4

23	24	25	26	
33	34	35		37
43		45	46	47
53	54	55	56	57
63	64		66	67
	74	75	76	77

1	2		4	5
	12	13	14	15
21		23	24	
31	32	33	34	35
	42	43		45
51		53	54	55

Appendix

Grid Paper

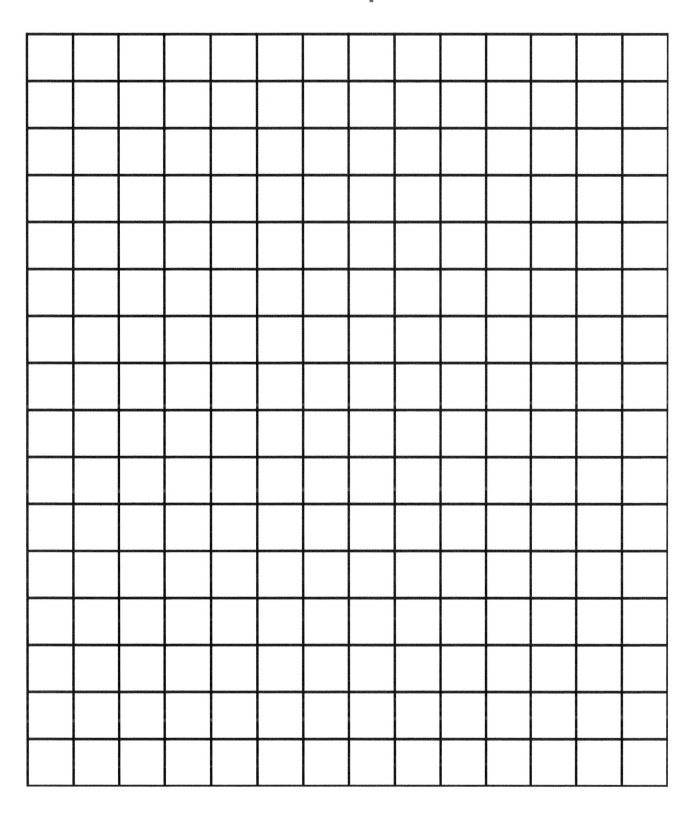

About the Authors

Dr. Jo Boaler is a professor of mathematics education at Stanford University, and the cofounder of Youcubed. She is the author of the first MOOC on mathematics teaching and learning. Former roles have included being the Marie Curie Professor of Mathematics Education in England, a mathematics teacher in London comprehensive schools, and a lecturer and researcher at King's College, London. Her work has been published in the *Times,* the *Telegraph,* the *Wall Street Journal,* and many other news outlets. The BBC recently named Jo one of the eight educators "changing the face of education."

Jen Munson is an assistant professor of learning sciences at Northwestern University, a professional developer, and a former classroom teacher. She received her PhD from Stanford University. Her research focuses on how coaching can support teachers in growing their mathematics instructional practices and how teacher-student interactions influence equitable math learning. She is the author of *In the Moment: Conferring in the Elementary Math Classroom,* published by Heinemann.

Cathy Williams is the cofounder and director of Youcubed. She completed an applied mathematics major at University of California, San Diego before becoming a high school math teacher for 18 years in San Diego County. After teaching, she became a county office coordinator and then district mathematics director. As part of her leadership work, Cathy has designed professional development and curriculum. Her district work in the Vista Unified School District won a California Golden Bell for instruction in 2013 for the K–12 Innovation Cohort in mathematics. In Vista, Cathy worked with Jo changing the way mathematics was taught across the district.

Acknowledgments

We thank Jill Marsal, our book agent, and the team at Wiley for their efforts to make these books what we'd imagined. We are also very grateful to our Youcubed army of teachers. Thanks to Robin Anderson for drawing the network diagram on our cover. Finally, we thank our children—and dogs!—for putting up with our absences from family life as we worked to bring our vision of mathematical mindset tasks to life.

Index

for, 22, 42–43; with discrimination, 49; from displays, 147; with dots, 144; with drawing, 164; with figures, 93; with focus, 199; free space for, 14; frustration in, 12; with images, 30; from investigation, 78, 136; with labeling, 27; from listening, 210–211; with magnets, 105; movement for, 28; from music, 203; neuroscience of, 3, 9–10; from observations, 54; with partners, 70, 151; with patterns, 45–46, 108–109, 220–221; perception for, 47–48; from pictures, 5–6; by play, 98; in real world, 44–45; from recognition, 67–68; recomposition, 118; recording and, 149, 221; with reference objects, 108; routines and, 79, 106; with rules, 180; in small-groups, 53; with squares, 137; with symbols, 169; tasks, 95–96, 127; terminology, 82; thinking and, 4–5; about triangles, 96; from visualization, 104; with wooden blocks, 137–140

Lines, 144–150
Listening, 141, 154, 210–211
Little Kids—Powerful Problem Solvers (Andrews/Trafton), 138
Lockhart, Paul, 8
Look-fors: building blocks, 100–101; count a collection, 27–28; counting larger collections, 210–211; DIY patterns, 198–199; dot talks, 108–109; feeling fingers, 54; foot parade, 154–155; growing bigger and bigger, 140–141; hand mirrors, 73–74; how many do you see?, 33–34; for hundred chart patterns, 222–224; kinder dance party, 203–204; make a shape, 95–96; making a collection, 217–218; making a counting book, 44–46; roll the dice, 147–149; show me with your fingers, 67–68; snap it!, 122; sorting buttons, 179–180; sorting emojis, 171; sorting supplies, 165–166; talking about shapes, 82; which is more?, 126–127; a world of patterns, 187–188

Low floor, high-ceiling tasks, 2–3, 14

M

Magnets, 105
Make a shape, 93–96
Making a collection, 213–218
Making a counting book, 40–46
Manipulatives, 17–19, 209, 213
Marshmallow challenge, 77
Masking tape, 19
Mason, John, 8
Matching, 126
Math. *See specific topics*
Mathematics, the Science of Patterns (Devlin), 181
Memorization, 2, 4–5, 21
Menon, Vinod, 9–10
Milich, Zoran, 41
Mini numbers, 12
Mistakes, 14, 166
Modeling, 101
Movement, 28
Muffin tins, 177–178
Music, 203

N

Negotiation, 15
Neuroscience, 2–4, 9–11, 14, 47, 103; investigation and, 182; of patterns, 201
Numbers: ANS, 103–104; CGI for, 138; combinations of, 153; composing, 151–155;

Stretching counting toward 100, 205–206

Structures, 15–16, 26, 45–46

Struggling, 27–28

Students: accuracy by, 154; approaches for, 22; attention of, 187, 199; big ideas for, 9; challenge for, 139; charts for, 118; collaboration by, 162; color-coding for, 49, 51, 220–221; conceptual engagement for, 28; construction by, 97; counting books for, 40; counting stations for, 23; creativity and, 93–94, 204; curiosity of, 21; data science for, 135–136; decisions by, 170; deductions by, 168, 171; descriptions by, 79, 101, 148–149, 179–180; drawing by, 124; encouragement for, 162; experimentation by, 77; exploration by, 161, 195; ideas by, 98, 197; investigation by, 14–15, 41, 174, 200; journaling for, 5–8; in kindergarten, 21, 205; labeling by, 31, 33–34, 73, 121, 164, 214; language of, 33; low floor, high-ceiling tasks for, 2–3; number lines for, 136; observations by, 72, 127, 138–141, 161, 184, 223; one-to-one correspondence for, 27; part-whole relationships for, 119; play for, 13–14; precision by, 45, 96; predictions by, 188; preparation for, 210–211; recognition by, 105, 122, 145; recording by, 100; routines for, 26–27; sharing by, 74, 95, 123, 151; sorting systems for, 165; strategies for, 137, 144; struggling by, 27–28; subitizing by, 147; tracking by, 54; visualization for, 9–13, 48, 65, 166; word choice by, 81–82; Youcubed summer camp for, 3–4, 11–12, 104

Subitizing, 105–106, 108, 144, 147–148

Surveys, 21

Symbols, 169

T

Talking about and making shapes, 77–78

Talking about shapes: images for, 84–92; instructions for, 79–83

Tasks, 3–4, 12, 95–96, 127, 169

Teachers: building blocks for, 98; count a collection for, 24; counting larger collections for, 208–209; displays by, 202; DIY patterns for, 196; dot talks for, 105–106; encouragement by, 54, 165–166, 178–179, 198; engagement by, 12; evidence for, 73; foot parade for, 152; growing bigger and bigger for, 138; hand mirrors for, 71; how many do you see? for, 31; hundred chart patterns for, 220–221; judgment of, 164; kinder dance party for, 201; labeling by, 107; listening by, 141, 154, 211; make a shape for, 94; making a collection for, 214–215; making a counting book for, 41–42; observations by, 26, 96, 126–127, 178, 180, 197, 203–204, 217; parents and, 47; recording by, 222; research for, 1; roll the dice for, 145–146; show me with your fingers for, 65; snap it! for, 119; sorting buttons for, 175–177; sorting emojis for, 169; sorting supplies